The
DARK NIGHT
of the SOUL

Out of the Darkness
and into the Light

MICHAEL MIRDAD

GRAIL
PRESS

THE DARK NIGHT of the SOUL
Out of the Darkness and into the Light

**GRAIL
PRESS**

PO Box 1908
Sedona, AZ 86339
(360) 671–8349

office@GrailProductions.com
www.MichaelMirdad.com

Book cover and interior design by
Lanphear Design

www.lanpheardesign.com

Library of Congress Cataloging-in-Publication Data
Mirdad, Michael.

The Dark Night of the Soul/
Michael Mirdad.

ISBN: 978-0-9855079-9-2

SECOND EDITION

Acknowledgments

Whom do I thank and acknowledge in a book about the Dark Night of the Soul? To me, it's clear that I want to thank everyone with whom I have ever crossed paths—especially those of you who came to me for a private session (spiritual counseling), as it is you (and God) who wrote this book. You may have been a challenging character in my life's drama, or you may have played the part of a supportive character. Either way, I thank you for revealing whatever it was that I needed to see on my way to the Light at the End of the Tunnel.

My heartfelt thanks go to Lynne Matous for her superb editing and to David Brown, Gregg Matous, Judy Messer, Matthew John, and the rest of my team of proofreaders: Terrie, Lena, Dosi, Linda Mae, Joan Belle, and Joy Nanda. Also, many thanks to Bob Lanphear for his continued brilliant book and cover design.

Table of Contents

FOREWORD

My friend had a dream. She was in a tunnel only wide enough she could easily touch both walls if she stretched out her arms. The passageway was lit by a distant bright white light, which also exuded a warm and enticing invitation. Her emotions were a mixture of eager expectancy and adventure clothed in raw excitement. That inviting light was her goal, and she was running toward it, joyfully consumed by anticipation.

Abruptly, it vanished, and everything went pitch black, the medium of dark that extinguishes all sense of space and distance. Even her hands became invisible, as if disconnected from her body. She stopped and froze, unsuccessfully reaching through senses other than sight for any perception of path. Even the memory of what seemed so clear a moment before began to fade and with it all sense of direction. Fear replaced hope, and she stood immobile, gripped by a growing sense of desperation and despair. What had given her a sense of purpose and drive had disappeared in an instant, and now darkness and fear wrapped round her like constricting chains.

This is where she stayed for an indeterminate time, unable to risk a step. She was stuck. Finally, she decided that this was no way to exist and that any choice was better than being locked in place by fear. Stretching out her arms, she was easily able to touch both tunnel walls and began to shuffle her way forward in the direction she had first been heading. Better any movement than none at all, even if it was in utter darkness.

Unexpectedly, her right hand lost contact with the wall; and feeling around, she discovered that there was a small opening and another corridor of some sort branching off to her right. Now she had to make a decision. Either continue in the dark toward the light that had originally given her a sense of purpose or take the risk of this new possibility. She made a choice; and turning from her original path, she entered the new one, slowly and arduously making her way. The tunnel took a few turns; and suddenly, ahead of her again, appeared the light. With it, a sense of hope and purpose returned; but instead of running, she now walked confidently forward, knowing that even if this light also went out, there would always be a path that would present itself. She realized that if the first light had not gone out, she would have run past the opening in the wall that would ultimately be her new path.

Over the years, this dream has spoken to many of my friends, especially as they have journeyed seasons of the Dark Night of the Soul. Such periods of time feel isolating; and one is gripped by a sense of aloneness, or as alone as anyone can be in the presence of only the Divine, one's self, and one's journey. In a world consumed by perfection and production, one is easily swept along by the tide of activity.

The motion itself can present as purpose and meaning, and if not aware, one can begin to attach a sense of identity to external forms and frantic endeavor.

Is not one of the great gifts of darkness an invitation to grow in self-awareness? It stops us in our tracks and slows everything down. So much of what surrounded us now becomes exposed as hollow temptations to meaning. We fight the Dark Night because we believe in our activity to define us, save us, and grant to us an identity. In the dark we must look elsewhere and within, and there we find our options are limited and simple; we can learn to trust or give in to despair.

Is there a greater Light than our own to which we belong? Is there a Love that knows us and pursues us with Relentless Affection? Is there meaning and purpose that will emerge, not from external options and activity, but from within our very beings as an expression of our union with the Divine?

The soul is the inside-house to which you belong and is truly your home. The intention of the Divine is the integration of your life and person into wholeness, so that the Way of your Being becomes an expression of the Truth of your Being. The Dark Night is where God works in secret, away from the frenetic activities of the day. With Divine kindness in the most precious places of the soul, God confronts you; and with your participation, carefully removes stains from an ancient and intricately crafted wedding dress, in order that your life may become a more authentic and whole expression of your union with Love.

There is a faith in you that is more precious than gold, which perishes. In the Dark Night of the Soul, you are now receiving the goal of this faith, which is the healing of your soul. So, precious ones, do not be disheartened or dismayed when suddenly the lights go off; for in the darkness, truth and light will become more obvious, and trust will be the path.

–**Wm. Paul Young**, author *The Shack, Cross Roads, Eve,* and *Lies We Believe About God*

INTRODUCTION

There is an old saying: "There are *two* things in life that we cannot avoid, death and taxes." But the truth is, the only two things we cannot avoid are *death* and the *Dark Night of the Soul*.

Although not everyone goes to college, or gets married, or has children, or gets divorced; **everyone (and I mean everyone) goes through the Dark Night of the Soul**—at one *time* or another, and at one *level* or another. In fact, we all go through it at least two or three times in our lives— each occurrence averaging a few years in length. However, the Dark Night of the Soul is one of the world's best kept secrets—in that everyone goes through it, yet almost nobody talks about it or even knows anything about it.

Nonetheless, the Dark Night of the Soul transforms our lives for the better, but only if we move through the process properly—going through each step with the highest level of consciousness and integrity possible. This process helps us to learn what it is in our lives that is outworn and no longer necessary. The Dark Night can also help us to develop the courage to release such things. And, **even though going through it feels quite challenging, nothing on Earth does more for our soul's growth.**

*The term "Dark Night of the Soul" . . . refers to the
kind of spiritual crisis that leads us from profound
unknowing to radiant transformation.*

–Mirabai Starr

Experiencing **the Dark Night of the Soul is like going
through a dark tunnel; our goal is to reach the "Light
at the End of that Tunnel."** The dark tunnel represents
every form of lesson, test, and unhealed wound (known
or unknown) held within our psyche. On a personal,
fundamental level, the Light at the End of the Tunnel
represents a better life that awaits us, here, in this lifetime.
On a grand, universal level, the Light represents God and a
calling towards a greater love and willingness to surrender
our lives to God's Divine Plan.

*Buffeted by gusts of chance or drenched by rains of
misfortune, I nevertheless direct my mind to look
always toward Thee.*

–Paramahansa Yogananda

The only reason I can teach, write, and speak of the
Dark Night of the Soul so thoroughly is because I have
gone through it a few times and have done so consciously
enough to understand it. And instead of minimizing
it as simply being a "rough patch" in life, my eyes were
opened; and I came to know that there is a purpose for

it all. So, instead of thinking of the Dark Night as being a "negative" experience, I came to understand that **it is a very necessary period of dismantling our former selves to make room for a new self to be born.**

Even though it's an invaluable process, I really had a hard time appreciating its value whenever I was going through the Dark Night of the Soul. But each time I emerged from it, I was a new and better person—usually on all levels. It helped me to integrate everything I've ever studied or experienced, which means I had become a better teacher, healer, counselor, father, partner, and overall a better person. Because of the lessons I've learned and integrated, the Dark Night of the Soul has been an invaluable process.

My first experience with the Dark Night of the Soul was during my childhood and involved not feeling connected, not belonging to my family, and not knowing where to go for help or for answers.

During my second experience (which lasted about five years), I was around the age of thirty and had moved to the Pacific Northwest. I went through a divorce and all the challenging aspects of such an experience: loss of partner, car, house, and so on. I was reduced to sleeping on a couch in my office and often feeling quite alone. Most people around me at the time never would have known what I was going through, because I still was functioning as a father, had responsibilities to uphold, and was continuing to go on successful tours and facilitating spiritual classes. Nevertheless, it was a very dark, confusing, and depressing period.

My third experience with the Dark Night was around the time I turned fifty and moved to Sedona, Arizona. The most challenging part lasted approximately a year, but the overall process seemed to drag on for several years. This time around, I had to deal with a new set of challenges—namely; personal attacks, pettiness, gossip, and the eventual loss of those who I thought were my closest friends. At times, the stress level was so intense that it took a temporary toll on my health, my body, and even my level of trust (to some degree).

The latter two of these three Dark Night episodes coincided with an astrological "Saturn Return" (confirmed in my astrology chart); however, the first one did not. Also, the most recent episode of the Dark Night *should* have, according to the "stars," ended a few years before it finally did. Apparently, although Saturn was done with me, the Dark Night was not. So, much to my dismay, the experience continued for an extra couple of years.

Each time I went through the Dark Night of the Soul, I did my best to remain aware of the process, kept my faith in God and myself, and walked the fine line between "surrendering" and yet *not* giving up. Consequently, I've come to understand that keeping our faith and not giving up are some of the best ways to deal with the Dark Night and enter the Light.

If you are willing to renounce the role of guardian of your thought system and open it to me, I [Christ] will correct it very gently and lead you back to God.

—A Course in Miracles

The goal of this material is not only to better understand and navigate the Dark Night but also to explain how to *reach* the Light at the End of the Tunnel, and how to bring that Light into the world and into the lives of others.

The Longing

It feels as if the most beautiful lover in the world had come into your life, wooed you with perfect poetry and electric kisses, promised you were the one, the one and only, and then disappeared in the middle of the night without a word.

But this is a lover who will never leave you.

The lover has only gone to prepare your wedding chamber. Soon your betrothal will be consummated, and in the sweetest way you could possibly imagine. No, far sweeter than that. Your ecstasy will catapult you beyond yourself. You are a mountain stream rushing toward the sea, which is your lover, rising joyfully to meet you.

But for now, you do not know this. You cannot know this. You know only unbearable yearning. You have forgotten that the longing itself is the answer to the longing. That in the very crying out for the Holy One, the Holy One is pouring himself into you.

—St. John of the Cross

PART I

The Dark Night
of the Soul:
*Our Personal
Crucifixion*

THE DARK NIGHT
OF THE SOUL

You're not going crazy. . . you're just waking up! And the name for this "waking up" process is "the Dark Night of the Soul." That's right . . . there's a name for the challenging periods in your life where you most feel lost, confused, betrayed, afraid, and exhausted.*

"The Dark Night of the Soul" (life's greatest transformational experience) is not a term that everyone recognizes, and yet we all know it quite well. That's because every person who has ever lived on this planet (to the age of an adult) has gone through it in some form.

The "Dark Night" is a period of our lives wherein our soul has decided that it's time for us to journey within, so we can discover which parts of us need to be healed, transformed, and/or released. It's an *internal* process designed to teach us humility, how to surrender to life's healing processes, and how to become a better (more evolved) person.

Everything that happens is either a blessing which is also a lesson, or a lesson which is also a blessing.

–Polly Berrien Berends

The Dark Night of the Soul can take many forms, manifesting at various times in our lives in similar ways, but also in ways that are unique to our age. For example:

Childhood: Adoption, abuse, school taunting, parents divorcing, being the child of parents with addictions

Youth and Young Adult: Accidents, divorce, broken bones, broken heart, job loss, moving households

Later Adulthood: Glands burning out, loss of partner, betrayal, loss of good health, loss of loved ones, menopause

It's not just *individuals* that go through the Dark Night of the Soul. Groups of people also go through it, such as families and friends, as well as cities, nations, and the entire human race. In the past, the Dark Night has globally taken the form of the Great Depression and the world wars. In America, it took the form of the terrorist attack on New York City. It has also taken the form of natural disasters in various towns or regions. Sadly, however, during such events, most people focus on the logistics and details of the event and miss the deeper meaning and lessons involved—which then, of course, means there is a greater likelihood of having to soon *repeat* the Dark Night, perhaps in a different form.

> *In solitude we have our dreams to ourselves, and in company we agree to dream in concert.*
>
> –Samuel Johnson

During the Dark Night, we often may wonder if it's possible that anyone in the universe could know what we are feeling and going through. And it certainly may seem evident that no one else has a clue. Well-meaning friends might offer some form of support when we are going through the Dark Night of the Soul, but in most cases, they have little to offer. All too often, although they've likely gone through their own version of the Dark Night, they probably weren't awake and aware enough to understand the greater purpose behind the process. Therefore, there is little they can offer of true value. This tends to cause us to pull away from everyone, as we go even deeper into ourselves—like a chrysalis—which is exactly where God wants us and where our soul needs to be—focused inward on transforming. We tend now to more easily throw up our hands in total surrender. Soon after, we will come to realize that **when we opened our arms, our heart also opened. And when our heart is open, it is a natural invitation to the Holy Spirit or "Divine Mother" aspect of God** (Who *does* understand) to come and fill us up with Its Divine Presence.

> *Man is never helped with his suffering by what he thinks for himself, but only by revelation of a Wisdom greater than his own. It is this which lifts him out of his distress.*
>
> –Carl Jung

As we journey through the Dark Night, **the experience is like navigating a seemingly dark and endless tunnel**. Therefore, it is helpful for us to know some of the symbolic characters and characteristics we will likely encounter along the way. For example, we can imagine that a tunnel like this might be similar to a maze, with numerous side-tunnels. These side-tunnels symbolize life's potential distractions, including the numerous distractions from our ego that would try to keep us from reaching the Light at the End of the Tunnel.

The overwhelming darkness within the tunnel of the Dark Night symbolizes our fears of facing our hidden inner selves. Additionally, the creepy shadows and critters we may see and hear as we wander along, symbolize the various hurtful people we may have met along our path of life. Our journey through the dark tunnel (of the Dark Night of the Soul) also might symbolically feature terrifying sounds of screaming and crying that we can hear but without seeing their source. These symbolize our unhealed wounds—wounds that seem to haunt us throughout our life but speak loudly when we are moving through this dark period of our life. **Seeing the dark tunnel as a spiritual obstacle-course that features several symbols of distraction can help to provide the right perspective to more easily pass this test of our soul**.

Going through the Dark Night of the Soul is like a major housecleaning or a corporate clean-out—except that it's our soul that's doing the cleaning. It's not because there is something "wrong" with us, or that we've *done* something "wrong." Instead, the soul is just saying, "You know, I've looked through your memories and I found little bits of issues (for example, lessons not yet learned) here and there and wounds not yet healed—all of which are holding you back. So we're going to do a thorough cleanse of whatever we can so that you can move forward into a better life." Our soul also says, "By the way, we have some good news and some bad news: **the good news is that the Dark Night will *not* actually kill you. The bad news, however, is that at times it might make you *wish* you were dead.**"

Sometimes we have to die a little in order to be reborn and rise again as a stronger and wiser version of ourselves.

–Unknown

There is an irony to it all, because **although the Dark Night of the Soul is not something we would ever wish upon ourselves or anyone else, it is, nevertheless, the most educational and transformational experience this earthly life has to offer.** In fact, nearly every mystic, spiritual master, and the heroes and heroines of mythology from around the world, reached their greatest heights and epiphanies after going through the Dark Night of the Soul.

In the Dark Night of the Soul, bright flows the river of God.

–St. John of the Cross

The Dark Night of the Soul is a purging process that calls us to release all that is unhealed or unnecessary— releasing all that is in the way of our highest good. The process is trying to help us release all that is not yet divine within us and bring us closer to our true divine expressions.

Even though this holy night darkens the spirit, it does so only to light up everything.

–St. John of the Cross

It's called the "Dark *NIGHT*," but it should have been called the "Dark *PERIOD* (or Dark *Years*) of the Soul," because it *never* lasts for just *one* night. It's a challenging *period* that generally lasts anywhere from one to three years, but sometimes can last even longer—possibly several years.

How long it lasts, however, is not under our control and is determined by what lessons we have to learn and how long it takes for us to learn them. And let's be clear about something: **nothing we do will end the Dark Night of the Soul—even one day sooner than it is supposed to end.** All we can do is change how we respond to it and ease the struggle by following the suggestions found in this book. In fact, not being able to make it go away is one of the main purposes of the Dark Night—because part of our test is to see how we respond to the experience and how we respond to not feeling in control of everything.

The endurance of darkness is the preparation for great light.

–St. John of the Cross

Again, **the intention behind our soul taking us through the Dark Night is to help us grow.** But the average human being doesn't see it that way, mainly because the process usually involves a significant amount of loss and change— neither of which do humans usually appreciate. So instead of being an excited participant, most human beings end up resisting, fighting, and denying the value of this process— which only tends to increase their level of pain during the experience.

If a person wishes to be sure of the road he's traveling on, then he must close his eyes and travel in the dark.

–St. John of the Cross

The Dark Night of the Soul is related to the greater opening of our heart. There are, in fact, lessons, tests, and initiations that correspond to *each* aspect, or chakra, of our being—the Dark Night corresponding to our heart-center. **Our heart is being opened to new concepts and beliefs.** For example, if we are parents that hold judgments about gender preferences, our child might turn out being gay. If we are racist, our child might date or marry a person of different color.

The bottom line is that our heart is going to be opened and transformed—either the easy way or the hard way—

taking us further out of judgment of self and others. **Our heart is going to either open by *unfolding* with love, gentleness, vulnerability, and humility or it's going to be *torn open* through loss, betrayal, devastation, and conflict.**

> *Pain insists upon being attended to. God whispers to us in our pleasures, speaks in our consciences, but shouts in our pains. It is his megaphone to rouse a deaf world.*
>
> –C.S. Lewis

As the pressure mounts, it's a very common thing to want to blame someone for our challenges—especially during the Dark Night. However, let's face it, we might *try* blaming God or others; but if we do, it affirms that the source of the problem is somewhere outside of us, which likely means we will never find a solution.

On the other hand, if the Dark Night *is* indeed brought about by *us* (our soul) as a means of learning valuable lessons that teach us how to be clearer, stronger beings; we will eventually come to realize that we have within us all that we need to properly respond to this period in our lives. We also have the power to choose how we *manage* such an experience.

Perhaps the most terrifying aspect of all, during the Dark Night of the Soul, is when we feel as though God Itself has turned Its back on us. And it might take us a while to come to the peace-based conclusion that there is *no way* the

Real God could, or would, turn Its back on *anyone*. During the times when we do not feel God's Presence, it's usually because our internal pain has distracted us from feeling and experiencing that Loving Presence and from connecting with God. Nevertheless, one of the amazing things we learn during this difficult time of not feeling God's Presence is that **instead of demanding that God meet us in the consciousness of our perceptions and problems, we will now move closer to the Consciousness of God.**

> *God, who is everywhere, never leaves us. Yet He seems sometimes to be present, sometimes absent. If we do not know Him well, we do not realize that He may be more present to us when he is absent than when He is present.*

> —Thomas Merton

*See the book: *You're Not Going Crazy . . . You're Just Waking Up!* by Michael Mirdad

2

THE ORIGIN AND DEFINITION OF THE DARK NIGHT

The "Dark Night of the Soul" is a term that was popularized by St. John of the Cross, and eventually other mystics as well—throughout time. It's actually referred to in ancient times, but not necessarily by *that* name. One of the main reasons we call this process the "Dark Night of the Soul" is because Jesus' dark period of mystical soul-searching took place in just *one night*—in the Garden of Gethsemane.

The *Dark* Night of the Soul is referred to as such, because **it defines a "dark" period in our lives that helps us to get in touch with our soul—at the deepest level**. The Dark Night of the Soul occurs when our soul decides to take us on a journey that is not about the usual, day-to-day tasks and challenges related to our *outer* life, but rather, is about the tests and lessons related to our *inner* life.

> *The Dark Night is more than a learning experience;*
> *it's a profound initiation into a realm that nothing in*
> *the culture, so preoccupied with external concerns and*
> *material success, prepares you for."*
>
> –Thomas Moore

This is not a period that focuses on the usual mundane things of life such as going to school, getting a job, getting married, having children, and so forth. Instead, the Dark Night of the Soul is a period when we might simultaneously lose our job, have health issues, find out our partner is having an affair, and perhaps lose our loved ones. It's when it seems like we are being faced with *numerous* challenges—all at once. And again, **it's not like we're simply having a bad day, but rather it's like we're having a bad life!**

Many mystics (such as St. John of the Cross, Saint Theresa and Saint Francis) have left records of their experiences with the Dark Night of the Soul. In fact, one could hardly earn the title of "mystic" without having consciously gone through the Dark Night experience. Those mystics throughout history who have gone through the Dark Night describe it as a process wherein our spirit is purifying the ego-self. For this reason, mystics are often seen in the same light as the alchemists of the Renaissance period, because the symbolism of the alchemical process is the same as that of the Dark Night of the Soul: **the lower self is purged until the transformational process is complete**. All we find remaining within ourselves is pure gold, the purified self. In this sense, the Dark Night of the Soul gives birth to the Phoenix within us, but only if we die well (to the ego self) and are courageous enough to truly rise from the ashes.

We must be willing to get rid of the life we've planned,
so as to have the life that is waiting for us. The old
skin has to be shed before the new one can come.

–Joseph Campbell

Again, experiencing the Dark Night of the Soul is like being taken into the old alchemist's crucible to have all of our dross, or extraneous feelings and beliefs, burned away and transformed into something more pure. It is life's version of the darkness before the dawn. It's like the dark side of the moon—cold and lonely. And yet, **there is no human experience that can teach us more, nor prepare us more, for the new life that comes to those who remain as centered as possible in faith and courage.**

3

THE FIVE STAGES OF THE SOUL-TRANSFORMATION PROCESS

The Dark Night of the Soul includes *three* stages—all related to our personal crucifixion (emptying our cup). *The Light at the End of the Tunnel*, on the other hand, includes just *two* stages—both being related to our personal resurrection (refilling our cup). All together, they total *five* stages—collectively referred to as the "Soul-Transformation Process." But since many people aren't conscious enough to resurrect immediately after their crucifixion, they only go through the first *three* stages, which are: 1) Dismantling, 2) Emptiness (which includes grief and depression), and 3) Disorientation. However, those who choose to *resurrect* would then go through the additional *two* stages: 4) Rebuilding and 5) a New Life.*

There is a gap that must be crossed between stages *three* (Disorientation) and *four* (Rebuilding). If we do not take the "leap of faith" to bridge this gap by learning to surrender, we will likely find ourselves recreating our old life by either forcing some pieces back together or recreating merely a newer version of the old life. If, upon reaching the rebuilding stage, we draw back or freeze, we will go in a circle and return to the first stage of the Soul-Transformation Process—only to be dismantled again. In other words, **trying to delay our lessons and growth simply ends up causing such lessons to become even more intense so that we are less likely to miss them next time around**. On the other hand, if we stay on course and move through all of the first three stages properly, we will cross the bridge of faith and progress to "rebuilding a new life."

> *Sustaining faith is what sets you through those Dark*
> *Nights of the soul when you don't know where to go*
> *or what to do, and it seems that you can't last another*
> *day…but because of your faith in God, you do.*
>
> –Joel Osteen

The **five stages of the Soul-Transformation Process are a symbolic movement of the soul through each of the five levels of human consciousness—physical, emotional, intellectual, intuitive, and spiritual**. These stages, in turn, symbolize a progression through each of the five elements— earth, water, fire, air, and ether. Therefore, the dismantling stage mostly affects our physical, material life. The emptying stage relates mostly to our emotions. The disorientation stage relates mostly to our mind and intellect. The re-building stage relates mostly to our heart, soul, and intuition. Lastly, the stage of creating a new life relates mostly to our spirit.

*See the book: *Healing the Heart & Soul* by Michael Mirdad

4

THE DARK NIGHT
OF THE SOUL IS A
NATURAL PROCESS

A good way to understand the Dark Night of the Soul is to recognize that it is a *natural* part of life and is happening all around us. What this means is that life and nature itself, have no problem following the natural course of events related to the Dark Night of the Soul. As many of us know already, **every aspect of life goes through three stages or cycles: life, death, and rebirth**.

1. Life/Honeymoon (Life as it was before the Dark Night)
2. Death/Honeymoon over (Dark Night of the Soul)
3. Rebirth/New stage of life and love (Light at the End of the Tunnel)

As can be seen, it's the *second* stage (death or honeymoon over) that really represents the Dark Night of the Soul. So, for example, when we begin having relationship challenges (or challenges with our job or anything else), we are going through the "Dark Night" (second stage) of that relationship. Ideally, we will then bring this issue and relationship to the third stage of life, which is the Light at the End of the Tunnel.

> *If a man is to enter the Divine union, all that lives in*
> *his soul [former self] must die, both little and much,*
> *small and great.*

–St. John of the Cross

Truth be known, during the entire journey and existence of the soul, the soul is going through its *own* version of these same three stages: Our arrival into the universe; our "fall" into the earth plane; and our eventual resurrection/ ascension back into paradise. But what this means is that from an overall perspective, **being on earth is the soul's equivalent of the second stage of life, the Dark Night of the Soul**.

So again, everything in life goes through the above stated three stages or cycles of living. Unfortunately, the only exception is with *us*, human beings. Humans have been given free will, and **we often *exercise* that free will to choose NOT to reach the stage of rebirth (third stage)— bouncing back—after experiencing a major change, shift, or death**—especially when it comes to an *emotional* or *circumstantial* form of death. Such misuse of our free will allows us only to make it to the *second* stage ("honeymoon" over), which is a limited outcome that is *not* natural, as it does not reach all of its *normal* (natural) three stages.

There are musicians, for example, who reach a certain pinnacle or success (stage one), then can't seem to get the magic back on their next album (stage two), and that's as far as they go—only to the second stage of loss (a death of sorts), but with no apparent ability (or choice) to resurrect (stage three). Even our beloved Beatles (who sang that "all we need is love") failed to reach the *third* stage (total healing) of their relationship with each other—together or apart. In fact, it would be difficult to find more than a handful of successful music groups that didn't end up breaking up when they went through the second stage of their relationship, which is, in effect, the Dark Night of the Soul.★

Yet, who can blame anyone for not getting back up after being knocked down during the Dark Night? After all, it's like a "psychological form of death." And there is no time in our lives that is more challenging.

Psychologically, then, the 'Dark Night of the Soul' is due to the double fact of the exhaustion of an old state and the growth toward a new state of consciousness. It is a 'growing pain' in the organic process of the self's attainment of the Absolute. The great mystics, creative geniuses in the realm of character, have known instinctively how to turn these psychic disturbances to spiritual profit.

–Evelyn Underhill

Even Jesus honored this process of stages when he warned the apostles to appreciate him while he was here (the first stage), because they would be in pain when he was gone (the Dark Night, or second stage). But Jesus basically reassured them that he would pray and hold a vision that they would all make it to the Light at the End of the Tunnel (the third stage).

Again, these three stages flow naturally across many aspects of life (examples seen below)—with the Dark Night of the Soul being found in the *second* stage and the Light at the End of the Tunnel being in the *third* stage:

- Time: past, present, and future
- Nature: life, death, and rebirth
- Outer Environment: dusk, darkness, and dawn
- Relationships: honeymoon stage, honeymoon over, potential new level of life and love (with or without our partner)
- Business and finances: income, loss, bouncing back (or possibly retirement)

An *emotional* death during the Dark Night includes things like heartbreak, ending of friendships, loss of a loved-one, and so forth. A *circumstantial* death includes things like our car getting wrecked, the loss of a job, a change for the worst in our finances, and so forth. In all such cases, we are meant, and equipped, to come back to life: we have what it takes to get up, dust ourselves off, re-focus, and bounce back better than ever. The trick is to not do so on our *own* fuel and guidance, but rather, in a state of surrender to God as a Guide into a better life. As the saying goes, "Not my will but Your [God's] Will be done!" And the Dark Night is perfect for helping us reach that state of surrender.

All too often, however, surrendering to God's Will (our true will) is not what happens. Instead, many people tend to become so lost and desperate that, instead of surrendering to God's Will and Guidance, they end up doing one of two things: 1) They remain broken and wounded, not having the will or energy to come back to life; or 2) They bounce back, but they do so under the will and guidance of their ego and/ or under the direction of misguided friends.

> *God has to work in the soul in secret and in darkness because if we fully knew what was happening, and what Mystery, transformation, God and Grace will eventually ask of us, we would either try to take charge or stop the whole process.*
>
> —St. John of the Cross

Surrendering to the Will (Love) of God is certainly *not* natural to our ego, but it is *indeed* natural to our soul.

*See the book: *Creating Fulfilling Relationships* by Michael Mirdad

5

THE SIGNS
AND SYMPTOMS

There are several signs and symptoms that indicate we are going through the Dark Night of the Soul, as opposed to merely having a "bad week." We all have moments when we feel challenged, stuck, ill, and so forth; or lose a job, relationship, or partnership. And any one of these, by themselves, can send us into a downward spiral of emotional pain and/or physical discomfort.

In normal years of life, we usually face only a few of these challenges at a time, and they usually (with some exceptions) last only days or weeks. During the Dark Night of the Soul, however, instead of having only a few areas of our life challenged, we often experience *most* areas being challenged— often with *all* of them occurring at the same time.

When we go through the Dark Night of the Soul, our energy levels often drop. We might lose weight in an unhealthy way (or *gain* weight if our glands swing out of balance from the stress). We often feel a lack of will to live. Men might experience erectile issues, while women might experience a drop in libido. And that's because, overall, the Dark Night is like a serious bout of depression. And it makes it even more challenging that all of this can last for years.

*The Dark Night of the soul is when you have lost
the flavor of life but have not yet gained the fullness of
divinity. So it is that we must weather that dark time,
the period of transformation when what is familiar has
been taken away and the new richness is not yet ours.*

–Ram Dass

The first thing to do when we are wondering whether
our challenges are part of the Dark Night of the Soul or are
merely a challenging period of our lives, is to ask ourselves
if it involves *many* areas of our lives or just one or two. The
next thing to ask ourselves is how long it has been going on.
**It's probably best to assume we are in the Dark Night
of the Soul *only* after we are sure that it has affected
numerous areas of our life and has already lasted at least
several months.**

**Below are the seven primary signs or symptoms (in
most cases *progressing* from one to another) of going
through the Dark Night of the Soul,** followed by an
elaboration of each listed item:

- Several areas of your life have fallen apart (been
  dismantled), such as health, work, friendships, and so
  forth.
- Usually it lasts for one to three years—minimum.
- You feel stuck (like you are in a rut) and possibly
  depressed.
- Nothing you try in order to repair your current
  condition is working.

- You might feel either like a failure or a hypocrite.
- You feel like you have lost faith in God or in the process of life.
- You feel like you are in a state of shock.

1. *Several areas of your life have fallen apart (been dismantled)*: The Dark Night of the Soul is unique from other challenging times in your life in that it usually involves more than one or two key areas of your life.

2. *Usually it lasts for one to three years—minimum*: If it's the Dark Night, you will have been experiencing it for several months—at the least.

3. *You feel stuck (like you are in a rut) and possibly depressed*: The Dark Night of the Soul tends to make you feel physically, emotionally, and mentally exhausted.

4. *Nothing you try in order to repair your current condition is working*: This is similar to feeling like you are in a rut; but instead of focusing on the feeling, this focuses on the exhaustion that comes because nothing you do to try to change your current circumstance seems to work. This often results in giving up on trying anything else to help your situation.

5. *You might feel either like a failure or a hypocrite*: Because you have been stuck for so long, you might feel like a failure. It's also common to feel like you are a hypocrite because, at this time, you might not appear to "have it together" as well as you may have thought or have portrayed to others.

6. *You feel like you have lost faith in God or in the process of life*: Once you start to feel like a failure or hypocrite, it's only a matter of time before your faith will be tested, usually resulting in having doubts about your spiritual beliefs.

7. *You feel like you are in a state of shock*: The state of shock that comes from being in the Dark Night of the Soul varies most in its timing compared to other items on the list. For some people, the shock of having their lives dismantled comes immediately. For others, the shock doesn't really set in until years have gone by. In some cases, the shock adds to feelings of depression; in other cases, we simply go numb—not knowing what to feel.

6

IT'S ALL AROUND US

If you think that you have never heard of the Dark Night of the Soul, it's probable that while the *term* may be unfamiliar to you, the *experience* is not. **The Dark Night is all around us, but many are not paying attention**. Not only have you likely gone *through* it, the *experience* of the Dark Night has likely been portrayed in some of your favorite movies and has certainly been sung about in some of your favorite songs. The theme of the Dark Night is found in the life stories of most people you know and/or admire. It is even featured in the lives of the most popular cartoon characters, such as Bambi or Rudolph the Red Nosed Reindeer.

The Dark Night of the soul comes just before revelation.
When everything is lost, and all seems darkness, then
comes the new life and all that is needed.

–Joseph Campbell

It's obvious that the Dark Night is the theme of a song or story if it features feeling lost—not just romantically, but rather lost in life itself. Or the song or story might feature a life that was going well, taking a turn for the worst (which evokes a major awakening), and then everything turns out possibly better than when it started. Many songs that feature these themes have stories behind them that tell of the composers, by their own admission, going through a very dark period in their own lives.

Here are several examples of movies that feature the Dark Night of the Soul in their themes:

A Little Princess
Clash of the Titans
Groundhog Day
Inside Out
Lord of the Rings
Rise of the Guardians
Star Wars
The Count of Monte Christo
The Shack
The 13ᵗʰ Warrior
What Dreams May Come

Here also are several examples of songs that feature the Dark Night of the Soul in their themes:

"Amazing Grace"—Various Artists
"Bitter Sweet Symphony"—The Verve
"Bohemian Rhapsody"—Queen
"Carry on My Wayward Son"—Kansas
"Closet Chronicles"—Kansas
"Dark Night of the Soul"—Loreena McKennitt
"Don't Let the Sun Catch You Crying"—Gerry & The Pacemakers

"Don't Give Up"—Peter Gabriel
"Even in the Quietest Moments"—Supertramp
"Everybody Hurts"—R.E.M.
"Fire and Rain"—James Taylor
"Gethsemane"—from Jesus Christ Superstar
"Hide in Your Shell"—Supertramp
"Higher Love"—Steven Winwood
"Holy Mother"—Eric Clapton
"In My Time of Dying"—Led Zeppelin
"I Still Haven't Found What I'm Looking For"—U-2
"(I've Been) Searching So Long"—Chicago
"Kyrie"—Mr. Mister
"Let it Be"—The Beatles
"Ordinary World"—Duran Duran
"Paradox"—Kansas
"Show Me the Way"—Styx
"Solsbury Hill"—Peter Gabriel
"The Long and Winding Road"—The Beatles
"The Story in Your Eyes"—The Moody Blues
"Valley of Pain"—Bonnie Raitt
"Wild World"—Cat Stevens

Whether we're an artist, politician, musician, grandparent, or mythological hero, *everyone* **has spent time going through the Dark Night of the Soul.** This includes Abraham Lincoln, Martin Luther King, Jr., Mother Theresa, and Mother Mary. But the list also includes you, your parents, and your grandparents. The only difference between each of us is how we handle this phase of life.

7

BIBLICAL REFERENCES TO THE DARK NIGHT

There are references to the Dark Night of the Soul in nearly every holy, mystical, and spiritual text. The sacred teachings from every culture on every continent include stories and lessons related to the Dark Night of the Soul. These teachings and texts include the struggle of Arjuna in the *Bhagavad Gita*, and of course, every story in mythology ranging from Norse, African, and Greek mythology to the mythologies of Asia, Europe, and the Americas.

The Bible makes several references to the Dark Night, such as:

"This too shall pass."
"Though I walk through the valley of the shadow of
   death . . ."
"And man will cry for death but death will not come."

Also, the whole theme of the 23rd Psalm (which was written during King David's Dark Night of the Soul) is that **despite the darkness we have to go through during this cleansing period, we need to focus on the Light of God at the End of the Tunnel** and affirm that nothing on earth (death, divorce, disease, etc.) has the power over us that we once thought it did.

And this word, yet once more, signifies the removing of
those things that are shaken, as of things that are made,
that those things which cannot be shaken may remain.

–Hebrews 12:27

Other Biblical references to the Dark Night of the Soul include Adam and Eve's expulsion from the Garden of Eden, the captivity and eventual release of the Israelites, Jesus' internal turmoil in the Garden of Gethsemane, and even the main theme of the Book of Revelation.

The entire Book of Job (found in the Old Testament) is about a man who has a good, abundant life, but ends up going through the Dark Night of the Soul and thus losing everything—family, home, health, and livelihood. But, **through deep soul-searching and a great deal of patience, Job emerges from his Dark Night and reaches the Light at the End of the Tunnel**—which leads him to a whole new life, far better than the one he had before. And although he lost many of his so-called friends and family members, he ends up receiving even more than he originally had. And this, too, is *our* goal.

8

THERE IS A
PROFOUND PURPOSE

What is the purpose behind the Dark Night of the Soul? In one sense, there *is* no purpose because, in reality, we are made in God's Image, and therefore, we need nothing—no tests, no healing, and no learning. But since we, as human beings, so clearly have forgotten our true identity *in* God (and as a *part* of God)—an amnesia that is confirmed by our choices to find flaws and judge ourselves and others—it's clear that **we need to remember our innate divinity and to heal our soul of all that seems unholy**. The Dark Night of the Soul exposes all such unholiness by tossing us right into the middle of it, so we can choose to release it—either the easy way or the hard way.★

> *Truth, like gold, is to be obtained not by its growth, but*
> *by washing away from it all that is not gold.*
>
> –Leo Tolstoy

The Dark Night of the Soul helps us to purge away our old, limiting patterns and beliefs so that we can make room for a new, expansive and unlimited life. So the Dark Night could be seen as a "soul-level healing process."

It's like a soul-surgery, which can involve fear, exploration, discomfort, release of the past, and eventually recovery and feeling born again—all of which lead us to an entirely new life—after we reach the Light at the End of the Tunnel.

Sometimes a life, like a house, needs renovating,
the smell of new wood, new rooms in the heart,
unimagined until one begins the work. One rebuilds
because the structure deserves a renewing.

–Doris Schwerin

There are many benefits of going through the Dark Night of the Soul, such as the following:

- It helps us to let go of old, unhealthy patterns and beliefs.
- It teaches us to integrate all that we once read, heard, thought, and spoke.
- It changes all that we once loved conditionally into unconditional love.
- It encourages us to learn and practice humility and surrender.
- It helps to develop divine patience.
- It teaches us to release all attachments to things of this world and limiting beliefs within our mind.

*See the book: *The Seven Initiation on the Spiritual Path* by Michael Mirdad

9

IT FEELS LIKE WE'RE BEING CRUCIFIED

The crucifixion and resurrection of Jesus (also in the form of ancient rituals such as those used by pagans and Freemasons) are powerful and accurate metaphors for the Dark Night of the Soul—followed by reaching the Light at the End of the Tunnel.

This is not to say, however, that *everyone* resurrects after the "crucifixion" experienced during the Dark Night. For example, one might go through a divorce and never truly heal or bounce back from that experience—choosing to never again love or trust anyone. The truth is, as already mentioned, many people remain dead in the sense that they remain wounded, distrusting, or feeling without hope or direction. In other words, they failed to see and experience the Dark Night as a source of lessons and cleansing; therefore, they failed to resurrect or come back to life and discover what new life awaits them. This demonstrates that the level of our resurrection (rebirth) is determined by the depth of our crucifixion (death).

Do you choose the crucifixion or the resurrection?
We are speaking of the willingness to die to who you
have been, to be born to who you are. Every breath
you take relives the crucifixion and the resurrection.
Each exhalation allows all that has been to die. With
inhalation, you are born again into this moment of
Now. Every moment offers the promise of God.

–Emmanuel's Book

To remain dead (crucified) OR to come back to life (resurrect) is a matter of choice. And every person must make this choice with each of life's challenges—large or small. But again, many people—because of old unhealed wounds and unmet expectations—choose *death* instead of *life*.

Do not think that Jesus only was crucified; everyone in
some way has his cross to bear daily. Those who try to
do good in this world know what it is to be crucified by
enemies. When one gives love and gets treachery and
hate in return, those wounds of the heart are sometimes
harder to endure than the wounds that injure only the
body. When misunderstood or mistreated, that is the
time to live by the divine example set by Jesus.

–Unknown

Ultimately, the Dark Night of the Soul does not bring messages or lessons that are easy, because life's *easy* lessons are often things we are open to hearing and learning. **The Dark Night, however, tends to bring to us the messages and lessons that we've been ignoring or refusing to pay attention to**—things we prefer not to hear or learn.

10

THE DARK NIGHT OF THE SOUL IS DEPRESSING

To say that the Dark Night can stir a bit of depression in us is somewhat of an understatement. It would be like saying that Attila the Hun was slightly irritable. The truth is, **the Dark Night can sometimes make us feel like we have descended into a surreal world: the darkest levels of loneliness, confusion, and despair**. And, in a sense, there's not a damned thing we can do about it. No amount of money, status, or achievement can lift us out of this dark state.

There are certainly moments when we will grasp for *any* lifeline we can find. However, no partner, friends, family members, nor even a legion of angels can "save" us—because **we are going through a necessary process—a process that our own soul has designed for us**. Unfortunately, when others can't save us, we often will shift gears and try pushing everyone away. But this too rarely helps, and therefore, amounts to little or nothing.

The Dark Night of the Soul can feel like a major depression or sometimes like an ongoing anxiety attack or both. **It tends to make us feel like we're dying inside, and we *are*; we are dying of the old to make room for the new**. Yet, the Dark Night is different from most forms of depression, which are often caused by our body chemistry or from PTSD (post-traumatic stress disorder). The Dark Night of the Soul, on the other hand, is rooted not in our body, but rather, in lessons related to our soul's growth. Furthermore, whereas depression is often described as being similar to having a dark cloud above our heads, **the Dark Night is like having a dark cloud oppressing us from all seven directions: above, below, in front, behind, to the right, to the left, and on the inside**.

As my psyche went through this process of reorganization, I experienced a time of profound disorientation and suffering, not unlike that of those suffering from mental illness. The Dark Night of the soul can be a lonely time. We may find it difficult to communicate with others. Our lives may look relatively normal or even pleasant from the outside but feel very different on the inside.

–Dan Millman

Unfortunately, while we're going through the Dark Night, instead of focusing on the Light at the End of the Tunnel, we may be distracted by the deep, dark thoughts and emotions that are haunting us—against which we often feel powerless. This is a time when some people even consider (or commit) suicide because the Dark Night seems so difficult and without end. The ironic thing is that when such people feel compelled to take their own lives, it's only because they feel like they are already dying—and they are—*internally*. But the human mind (when hijacked by the ego) so often takes something it is feeling *internally* and compels us to act it out *externally*. It must be emphasized, therefore, that **when we *are* going through the Dark Night of the Soul, it's imperative that we continually remember to connect with God (and various human systems of assistance) for support and to remind ourselves that this experience has no real power over us**—as "This too shall pass!"

11

WHEN SATURN RETURNS

Astrologers often equate the Dark Night of the Soul with something called a "Saturn Return." And although we can experience a Dark Night that *doesn't* correlate with a Saturn Return, it often *does*. For example, we might have a couple of Saturn Returns in our lifetime, and yet we might have four or five Dark Nights of the Soul that are *not* synchronized with our astrological Saturn Return.

A Saturn Return is a time when the planet Saturn re-enters a significant part of our astrological chart—which means that it also returns as a significant period of our lives. Saturn is the name the Romans gave to the deity the ancient Egyptians called "Set," and the Christians later called "Satan." Needless to say, despite the common misinterpretations around such symbols of evil throughout history, when Saturn/Set/Satan enters our lives, it may seem like they make us go through hell, but there is another way of looking at this. **Saturn is a symbol for our ego-selves**, the part of us that remains separated and unhealed. Therefore, Saturn merely brings up the fears and suffering that already reside within us. Knowing how to handle a Saturn Return, therefore, can help us know how to deal with a Dark Night of the Soul.

Suffering seems like a tombstone around our neck,
while in reality it is only the weight which is necessary
to keep down the diver while he is hunting for pearls.

–Unknown

Although we may not like the idea of Saturn returning into our lives, there's nothing that takes us deeper into our personal wounds and lessons, which is why Jesus said, "You can only rise as far as you are willing to fall." Saturn, therefore, enters our lives merely to help us to see more clearly that which remains unhealed, or is in need of transformation.

12

THE EFFECTS ON OUR
BODY AND HEALTH

Since it is believed that *stress* is the main cause of nearly every ailment, and since the Dark Night of the Soul can be quite stressful, then it stands to reason that **the Dark Night is behind many of life's ailments**. Going through the Dark Night can cause an immunity breakdown, digestive issues, glandular problems, as well as any number of symptoms ranging from hair loss to ulcers—some of which may have a sudden onset, but also can accumulate over time.

Needless to say, experiencing the Dark Night of the Soul (ruled by the planet Saturn) is possibly the most stressful time in our lives, thus possibly taking a major toll on the health of our glands and the rest of our body. Saturn tends to increase the aging process—slowing down healing processes and speeding up death. Saturn slows down our digestive process and hardens our joints and tendons, possibly making us feel rigid and unable to move freely. Saturn also creates a restricting effect on our circulatory system, which results in the obstruction of bodily fluids, such as blood, lymph, urine, and even nervous energy.

Saturn is also linked to our skin and bones. The skin is our basic protective mechanism against the outside world, and during the Dark Night, we tend to feel more defenseless. Our bones represent our foundation, so when Saturn afflicts our bones, we feel like our foundation is crumbling.

There can be no rebirth without a Dark Night of the soul, a total annihilation of all that you believed in and thought that you were.

—Vilayat Inayat Khan

With all of this in mind, it should be clear that Saturn plays a huge part in our health and wellness. And **when Saturn is wreaking havoc in our lives and in the systems of our body, it should be no surprise that our body and health will show signs accordingly**.

We cannot heal what we cannot see. We cannot evolve if we cannot see. The Dark Night to me allows us to see what we otherwise could not see, as it will bring the deepest often most rejected aspects of our being into consciousness: our fear, our rage, areas where we lack acceptance, of illness, of suffering, of God, our ego identification.

—Unknown

One of the ways the Dark Night takes a toll on our body, is in relation to our endocrine system. Unfortunately, the materially-focused medical profession has difficulty understanding the true function of the endocrine glands and how to heal them because these glands are the most *spiritual* part of our *material* body. **So until the medical profession's viewpoint expands to include a *spiritual* viewpoint, the average medical professional will not fully understand our spiritual anatomy**, which includes these glands.

To increase our understanding of our glands (in relation to the Dark Night), imagine that the pituitary and pineal glands are like the Father and Mother aspects of God, and the thyroid gland, on the other hand, is like the Christ. Just as God (our Master) governs all love and life in creation, so too does the pituitary gland (our master gland) govern all the communication and metabolism in our body. Furthermore, **just as God uses the Christ to bring love to the world, so too does the pituitary use the thyroid gland to bring wellness and a healthy metabolism to our body**. In other words, the pituitary, pineal, and thyroid glands work together just as God and the Christ work together.

The thyroid is referred to as the Christ gland (center/chakra) because it is the *third* chakra and gland in our upper set of three chakras (symbolizing the Trinity of God) and is the *fifth* chakra and gland (counting upwards from the root center). This *fifth* position symbolizes the five-pointed star—the symbol of Christ. Every time we fail to honor our Christ Self in this world, however, our Christ gland—the thyroid—takes a hit. So **we keep killing (crucifying) the Christ in ourselves and each other by over-taxing the thyroid—which is the symbol of the Christ in our body**—with physical, emotional, and energetic toxins.

One of the most common ways we toxify our thyroid and our spiritual (Christ) Self is when we use our spoken "I AM" words in a way that does not reflect the Christ Truth. When we speak with hate, gossip, and negativity about our self or others, it crucifies/kills the Christ (our

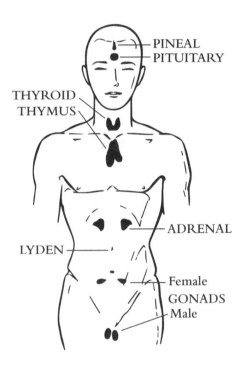

Christ spirit). And when the Christ grows weary, it soon is no longer the Christ and instead becomes the human self that is subject to every form of limitation—including illness. For this reason, accumulated, non-Christ experiences take a toll on the body, and the thyroid then becomes imbalanced, thus sending all of our physical world/glands into chaos. In other words, we betray ourselves and others when we improperly use our speech (or throat-center), which is connected to our thyroid—all of which can be reversed if/when we initiate the miracle of allowing our Christ Self to shine through our thyroid and every other part of our being.

13

TEN THINGS TO DO

When we're going through the Dark Night of the Soul, there are definitely things we *should* and should *not* do to help ease the process and possibly lessen its need to return.

To begin with, imagine the Dark Night as being like winter: if it's extremely cold out, we can prepare for it and dress accordingly. We also have the option of staying inside a bit more and enjoying warm baths. Or we might read and learn, and maybe even pray and meditate more often. The same is true when we are going through the Dark Night of the Soul—it is very much like being in the middle of one's personal, *internal* winter.

Metaphorically, **the Dark Night also can be like a period of hibernation—a period of going within**. But there are other times when it's more like we're being dragged out into the streets and towards a local hill to be crucified—which adds to our tendency to resist and/or fight the process— thus delaying its conclusion or calling it back to us yet again at a later date. It's not that we should completely lose our will to exist, or even our right to fight back on occasion. But we do need to learn to receive Guidance as to when we need to step-up, and when we need to let go.

THE DARK NIGHT OF THE SOUL

Surrendering to the Dark Night process does not mean becoming excessively passive, but it *does* mean learning to let go of attachments more easily. **And since it doesn't do us much good to keep trying to avoid the Dark Night process, we might instead ask ourselves what we can do to best deal with it**.

Here are ten things we should consider doing that can help us while going through the Dark Night of the Soul:

1. **"Die well."** This means that instead of fighting the process (crucifixion), we can learn to embrace it. This is not the same as "giving up." To "die well" means that if this process is calling us to go within, then let's go within and do a personal inventory of our unhealed wounds while we are there. And if it calls us to surrender things from our lives that are no longer serving us, then we can make a thorough list of what it's time to bid farewell to (including people, places, and things) and begin letting them go.

2. **Keep a casual attitude about the process.** Instead of thinking and speaking about it as a *horrible* experience (even though it might actually feel that way), we can treat it as lightly and naturally as possible.

3. **Feed your soul.** This means watching movies and listening to songs that lift our spirit. It's also okay to watch and listen to ones that make us cry—as long as we do not allow them to drag us down beyond our ability to rise again. Also, we can use prayer and affirmations.

Pray and affirm: "This too shall pass!" Or try, "There is only one Presence and one Power in my life, and that is God. Therefore, none of these challenges have any power whatsoever over me!"

4. **See a counselor.** Sometimes, friends will come in handy as sounding-boards. But often, during such a process as the Dark Night, our "friends" are long gone. Therefore, when going through such a deep and challenging time, it's important to talk about it with someone we trust— such as a counselor or sponsor.

5. **Do inner work.** Going through the Dark Night is a crucial time to look at our deepest issues and patterns. This is a time of the hero's journey, which means that if nature has drawn us inside, we might as well clean house. Journaling is a great way to bring issues out in the open for inspection, as well as a good way to process feelings—possibly gaining new insights.

6. **Watch for signs**. It's not to say we should become obsessed with every little sign and synchronicity. But during the Dark Night, it's important to remain open and prayerful for signs that might direct and guide us through the process and beyond.

7. **Come back to life**. Although there might be a period of mourning for the loss of a loved one, or even parts of ourselves, we are meant to resurrect from the dead and come back to life. So although a portion of the Dark

Night might be to "die well" (to what no longer serves our true self), there's also a portion (the Light at the End of the Tunnel) when we are meant to come back to life and begin moving forward.

8. **Remember that Christ told us there would be challenges in this world**. Christ told us not to sweat it because he has already overcome the power this world seems to have over us. And if fear seems to become overwhelming, we can call upon Jesus or God or our angels and trust that they will come to support us, and with them comes all the power of Heaven.

9. **Remember the purpose for going through the Dark Night of the Soul**. It's trying to teach us humility, surrender, unconditional love, the value of letting go, and how to integrate everything spiritually, as well as healing in a way that may have once been merely a theory.

10. **Give thanks!** It's important to understand that we are not *asked*, nor *expected*, to give thanks for harm and trauma. What we give thanks for is what we can *learn* from such events.

(14)

TEN THINGS TO
AVOID DOING

Besides a list of things to *do* during the Dark Night period, there are also ten things we should *not* do while going through the Dark Night of the Soul:

1. **Don't take the process personally.** This is not being done *to* you; it's being done *for* you.

2. **Don't give up.** Despite how you feel, there is no need to cave in and let this get the best of you. So stay afloat until you can rise above such emotions, but never, ever allow yourself to sink too far, nor give up. Besides, it's virtually impossible to have to deal with more than you can handle, and you are not expected to do so.

3. **Don't bother asking, "Why me?"** It's not that you're a bad person for asking this, but it won't do you any good to feel like a victim or to shame yourself.

4. **Don't blame God.** God has nothing to do with it. The Dark Night of the Soul is the Dark Night of YOUR soul. All the lessons and challenges are coming from within your *own* soul's belief-systems.

5. **Don't bother making a lot of plans**. Trying to launch projects while you're in the midst of the Dark Night is like rearranging the deck chairs on the Titanic. It's also like having your tires deeply stuck in a muddy rut yet continuing to accelerate and spin your tires, which only causes you to dig-in more deeply. Certainly there's something here and there that might still work out all right, as life does go on. But, for the most part, it's not wise to put a lot of energy or investment into expecting things to reach fruition at the present time. Put another way, this may be the appropriate season to *plan* a new garden, but perhaps not the best time to actually *plant* the new seeds for the garden.

6. **Don't get overly invested in expecting the Dark Night to go away**. Like many other things in life, the Dark Night may drag on a bit longer than you expected. So don't get overly invested in its ending.

7. **Don't allow yourself to doubt your progress**. Just because some personal issues (or perhaps old wounds) are beginning to surface during the Dark Night, does not mean you were somehow mistaken to ever think you healed such issues. The Dark Night is notorious for magnifying things, which means that even tiny remaining bits of your issues can sometimes look magnified enough to give you the impression that, when it comes to your personal healing, you are not getting anywhere after all. However, this is *not* necessarily true.

8. **Don't give in to potential addictions.** Be careful not to give-in to the temptation to mask over your current feelings with any form of addiction—drugs, alcohol, nor even things like food.

9. **Don't take your pain—your fears, anxieties, and frustration—out on anyone.** It's important to be as responsible as possible; otherwise, your actions could cause irreparable damage.

10. **Do NOT attempt to "go it alone."** Remember that one of the main purposes for this experience of the Dark Night is to teach you to be more humble and to come more closely to Spirit/God. Even if you are neither spiritual nor religious, you can still choose to surrender—in your own way—all of your hurt and challenges by simply saying, "I need help and I am open to any such help." Then patiently watch and see, as well as feel, any shifts that might occur—even if ever so subtly. Then verbally give thanks for those shifts.

15

ASSISTING OTHERS THROUGH THE DARK NIGHT OF THE SOUL

As any wise man or woman knows, we are *not* here on Earth merely to fulfill our own personal goals and aspirations. **We are here to learn and grow in consciousness. But we also are here to share our growth and consciousness with others.** And one of the most valuable places to share such gifts is with those who are going through the Dark Night of the Soul. During such a period, the recipient of the Dark Night could use our help, love, and support. And just as there are specific things that we can do to ease the suffering of the Dark Night for ourselves, there are also specific things we can do to assist others.

> *I am here only to be truly helpful.*
>
> *—A Course in Miracles*

If we encounter others who are going through the Dark Night, the most important thing to convey is that it's quite normal. In other words, we should help them feel and understand that they're not going crazy . . . they are just waking up. We can offer encouragement, using words that they can relate to, as we offer love and support, which helps to bring light to that dark place. The Dark Night can sow many wonderful seeds of growth for the recipient, but it still can be quite a painful process. Therefore, since we can't totally alleviate their pain, the least we can do is to support them with loving kindness through this challenging time.

Do not withhold good from those to whom it is due,
when it is in your power to help.

–Proverbs 3:27

We can let them know that whatever they are going through is just a *phase* and that "This too shall pass." It's so healing for people to hear these words. Perhaps we can say, "Guess what? I know you're going through major challenges right now, and I know how difficult and multilayered it is. Did you know there's a name for it? It's called The Dark Night of the Soul. Jesus went through it. Buddha went through it. Mother Teresa went through it. Mother Mary went through it. I've gone through it and you're going to go through it. It's a very *common* (but usually ignored) experience in life that is intended to help us in our awakening and becoming better people." Such words can really benefit others because it helps them feel "normal," and it eases their temptation to feel alone and to take the process personally.

As we ease the hearts and minds of others going through the Dark Night, we too are lifted to new levels of understanding, which in turn will help us the next time we make this journey toward the Light at the End of the Tunnel.

> *The truly helpful are God's miracle workers, whom I [Christ] direct until we are all united in the joy of the Kingdom. I will direct you to wherever you can be truly helpful, and to whomever can follow my guidance through you.*
>
> *—A Course in Miracles*

16

BRINGING THE DARK NIGHT TO A CLOSE

As previously mentioned, we cannot bring an end to the Dark Night of the Soul any sooner than it's designed to end—designed by our soul's contract with it. And *technically* this is true. However, **although we may not be able to *end* the experience *completely*, we certainly can** *change* **the experience.** This involves not only a change in perception—mostly accomplished through prayer, healing, and forgiveness—but also involves creating some major changes in our environment. This, then, tends to create shifts in our outer circumstances.

Changing our circumstances does not mean *forcing* changes. However, it *does* mean becoming centered enough to receive Guidance about changes we *can* make in order to assist the Dark Night to a smoother close or transition. We then need to implement this Guidance into our lives. This way we are shifting things—inside and out.

> *Change what you can and accept what you cannot.*
>
> −Paraphrased from the 12 Step Program

During the Dark Night period, many aspects of our lives are either collapsing or are stuck, which, in most cases, means we're most likely not going to have much success getting anything to change. Nevertheless, there is a "secret" method—unknown to most people—that can stir up some change. Of all the possible techniques we can use at this time to evoke a shift in an otherwise dark scenario, one of the best options is a technique we might call "stirring the ethers." This involves knowing that although we might not expect *too* many major improvements during the Dark Night, we can, however, take appropriate steps to change the energy of our situation by getting some things moving. In other words, we will "change whatever we can," and of course "accept whatever we cannot change."

The "secret" technique of *changing what we can* rests on having the courage to step in and assist the Dark Night with its attempt to remove all that is unnecessary from our lives. In other words, it's time to clean house, sell some things, give some things away, and throw some things away—all of which should be done with a spirit of feeling free and inspired, not depressed. It helps if we play our favorite music, spray some pleasant aromas, open the curtains, and start letting things go. The more thorough we are in this cleansing, the more effective we will be at *stirring the ethers* to create a change. And although we may or may not see immediate effects, we often will feel a little lighter and more free.

One thing is certain, however, we will have made more room for the light of our new life to enter—which might manifest as feeling better. Or perhaps we will receive new insights as to the next steps toward our new direction. **Even though it may not be time yet to completely come back to life (resurrect), we certainly can speed-along the death of our old life (crucifixion).** And although humans *cannot* speed up the process of the Dark Night of the Soul, "masters" *can*, and we are all masters in the making.

Again, although we can't actually *force* or *rush* the new life, we *can* be responsible enough to clean house (literally and figuratively) to make room for that new life. Making room may involve fasting to lose weight, getting a colonic to cleanse our system, having leaves and debris removed from our yard, and so forth. Even though our new life may not come rushing in, we *can* expect the old life to disappear a bit faster, which makes room for the new life to enter more smoothly and possibly even a little sooner.

> *Sometimes the only way for me to find out what it is I want to do is to go ahead and do something. Then, the moment I act, my feelings become clear.*

> –Hugh Prather

This idea of changing what we can is somewhat similar to that of "patching leaks" when we stand in the Light at the End of the Tunnel (covered in the second part of this book). However, the technique of "changing what we can" focuses mostly on "releasing the *old*." "Patching leaks," on the other hand, focuses mostly on "making way for the *new*."

"Changing what we can" involves courageously picking ourselves up—even during our darkest time—and finding some constructive things we can do—particularly related to cleaning our old boxes, attics, closets, and so forth. "Patching leaks," on the other hand, involves fine-tuning or releasing old beliefs and/or projects that might still be lingering with us, unconsciously inhibiting the flow of the new. Even if we have moved into the Light at the End of the Tunnel, we still may need to patch some leaks that are undermining our movement into a new life.

Again, one of the best tools for *changing what we can* involves cleansing (cleaning out) our mind, body, and soul. Whenever we do a responsible and thorough cleansing of the old or the past, a shift happens. Even though we may still seem (or feel) so stuck during the Dark Night, **making significant changes in our soul and our environment break up the stagnation in order to allow the flow of fresh energy and inspiration**.

> *Forget about what's happened; don't keep going over old history. Be alert, be present. I'm about to do something brand-new. It's bursting out! Don't you see it? There it is! I'm making a road through the desert, rivers in the badlands.*
>
> –Isaiah 43:18-19

Since the Dark Night of the Soul is a period in our lives when many things seem to be taken away, **one thing we**

can do to ease the struggle of losing everything is to leave nothing left to be taken. In other words, it's "purge or be purged"! So, one of the best ways to prepare for, and go through, the process is to make a list of all the things that *have* been taken, or are in the *midst* of being taken, or are *stuck* (going nowhere) and, therefore, *should* be taken. This can be followed by doing a "goodbye ceremony," bidding farewell to each of the items on the list (people, dreams or things) one at a time. This ceremony might evoke tears, laughter, anger, relief or any number of other emotions. However, it is wise not to resist any of these emotions, and instead to just let them flow in whatever form is appropriate—given your surroundings.

> *In order to arrive at having pleasure in everything,* [we must] *Desire to have pleasure in nothing. In order to arrive at possessing everything,* [we must] *Desire to possess nothing. In order to arrive at being everything,* [we must] *Desire to be nothing. In order to arrive at knowing everything,* [we must] *Desire to know nothing.*

> –St. John of the Cross

When we are bidding farewell to the items on our lists for purging, it is not to be done with an attitude of *failure*. Instead, it is to be done with a recognition that this item is either *gone*, *going*, or is *stuck*. As we release such things, it helps to remind ourselves that any inspiration or energy that was left in them is certain to be recycled—either into a different form or into something *completely* new. Either way, releasing them can *only* result in something better—and for our highest good—especially if we are open to perceiving it that way.

Once we are certain that we have done all we can to create a change in our circumstances, likely lessening the intensity of the Dark Night, we must "let go and let God"— meaning we have to release the outcome to Divine Order. **Although we will likely see some positive results from these suggestions, whenever there is a lack of change (especially after doing everything possible to "change what we can"), it's time to "accept the things we cannot change."** We accept them as they are and try to come to peace with them. Such accepting is empowering, not failing, if we but choose to see it from the proper perspective.

If anything we do works to facilitate the close of the Dark Night, that's great! But it's vital that we not become attached to the outcomes, as such attachment is a negative form of trying to manipulate the universe. These challenging circumstances (which may include relationships, objects, habits, and/or our jobs) will change eventually—in their own time.

After all of the above is put into practice, we usually can see some shifts—either *minor* shifts that help us *feel* better as we continue our journey through the Dark Night OR *major* shifts that actually help us to take our final steps out of the darkness and into the Light (at the End of the Tunnel).

A Creed for Those Who Have Suffered:

I asked God for strength that I might achieve . . .
I was made weak that I might learn humbly to obey.
I asked for health that I might do greater things . . .
I was given infirmity that I might do better things.
I asked for riches that I might be happy . . .
I was given poverty that I might be wise.
I asked for power that I might have the praise of men . . .
I was given weakness that I might feel the need of God.
I asked for all things that I might enjoy in life . . .
I was given life that I might enjoy all things.
I got nothing that I asked for . . .
but everything I had hoped for.
Almost despite myself, my unspoken prayers were answered.
I am among all men most richly blessed.

–Unknown Civil War Soldier

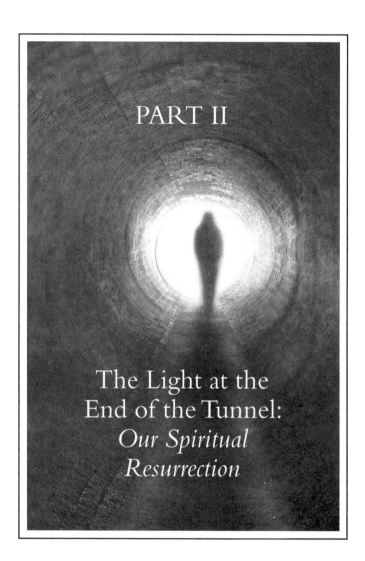

PART II

The Light at the End of the Tunnel:
Our Spiritual Resurrection

17

THE LIGHT AT THE END
OF THE TUNNEL

When it's time to emerge from the Dark Night of the Soul, how high we soar into a new life depends on a few things: **how well we did with our tests, how much we surrendered and kept our faith, and how deeply we allowed ourselves to heal during the process.** Some of the gifts our new life may feature can include greater happiness, an increase in prosperity, and healthier relationships, to name just a few. Other gifts might include writing a book, being inspired to launch a new career, experiencing an improvement in health, meeting new (better) friends, and the list goes on.

New beginnings are often disguised as painful endings.

–Lao Tzu

But first we have to deal with residual feelings of the Dark Night—a period in our lives when part (or possibly all) of our life is dismantled, leaving us feeling empty and disoriented. **It's time now to begin clearing away the disorientation and moving forward with co-creating**

a new life. However, this disorientation might still linger for a while, thus further delaying any major changes, which is why, during this time, we tend to ask ourselves specific questions about life, such as:

"Now what?"

"Is my life over?"

"Where have all my friends gone?"

"Who's left that I can trust?"

"Since who I thought I was is no longer true, then who am I?"

"Now what am I supposed to do with my life?"

And it's best *not* to answer such questions right away, as the dust (from our life's demolition) has not yet completely settled. But when it truly is time to answer, it's better not to answer with the voice of the little self—the ego—but rather to allow the Voice of *God* to reveal the answer.

Now that we've emptied the old contents of our cup (during the Dark Night of the Soul), God will refill that cup (while we reside in the Light at the End of the Tunnel). But **if we want something new in our life, it's necessary to set aside *previous* learning and experiences that conflict with the *new* awareness of who we truly are**.

> *To him who overcomes . . . I will give . . . a white stone, and a new name written on the stone.*
>
> –Revelation 2:17

As our new life emerges, it may not look familiar (which can be a little scary), but ultimately, that's probably a good thing. Now that we've been through varying degrees of a personal hell, it's time to realize that life is not about trying to control our own destinies. Instead, it's time for us to "get out of the way." **This is a time for rejuvenation and for receiving Guidance for our next steps**, followed by implementing these new ideas and inspirations.

> *The heaviness of being successful was replaced by the lightness of being a beginner again, less sure about everything. It freed me to enter one of the most creative periods of my life.*
>
> –Steve Jobs

Although we have reached the Light at the End of the Tunnel, and seem ready to "turn the corner" and enter a new life—it must be a life built *not* with human minds or hands. **Instead of trying to take control, now is the time to be still and allow God to inspire whatever new direction is best for our highest good**. It's time now for more prayer, meditation, and affirmation of the Truth and Power of God. As *A Course in Miracles* advises, "Make it a habit to ask for help where and when you can; you can be confident that all wisdom will be given when you need it."

And although the Dark Night of the Soul may have left us feeling lost and empty, the good news is that **we are**

THE DARK NIGHT OF THE SOUL

now more teachable and ready for our lives to be filled up again. At this point, most people will settle for being filled with just about anything. They have been hurting and longing for so many months or years, they will settle for any form of distraction (new or old) that comes along. But for those of us who are more aware (awake)—we know that settling for merely *anything* that comes along is what took us into some of the most painful layers of the Dark Night in the first place, and we don't want to repeat that. **So instead of jumping off the deep end by following rash ego-compulsions, it's best if we choose to move slowly at this time and wait for Guidance from Spirit**. Now is the time to avoid repeating old patterns of choices and behaviors. Instead, it's time to open our hearts, our minds, and our arms to God and ask to be Guided as never before. In other words, instead of trying to control our lives, it's now best to surrender to God and to become a co-creator of a new life.

> *It is only when everything, even love, fails that with*
> *a flash, man finds out how vain, and dream-like this*
> *world is. Then he catches a glimpse . . . of what's ahead*
> *and beyond. It is only by giving up this world that the*
> *other* [new world] *comes, but never through*
> *holding on to this one.*

> –Vivekananda

But how do we know when it's finally time to move forward, yet avoid the temptation to create our new life prematurely or on "the rebound?" There is no *one*, linear answer to this because each person's circumstances are different. This situation is not too dissimilar from having a terrifying nightmare in the middle of the night and waking up too scared to go back to sleep. So we lay in bed, feeling paralyzed by what has happened to us and wondering if the fear and trauma will ever subside. Then, before we know it, the view outside the bedroom window is no longer quite as dark, and we begin to hear birds chirping. Imagine the sense of peace and reassurance that comes over us. Similarly, **the way to know that the Dark Night has passed, and that we are entering the Light at the End of the Tunnel, is by watching for signs of a shift in our feelings, experiences, and outer circumstances**.

18

THERE'S LIFE AFTER
DEATH AFTER ALL

lthough it may seem hard to believe, **there *is* life after physical and psychological death**. So if we "weather the storm," hold our center, and emerge with our head held high (at least as high as possible) we can emerge from life's greatest crucifixion just as a butterfly emerges from its cocoon or the Phoenix rises from the ashes of its former life.

Each night, when I go to sleep, I die. And the next morning, when I wake up, I am reborn.

—Mahatma Gandhi

Despite the many times the Dark Night makes us feel blasted, wounded, and wanting to give up, Spirit calls to us: "Lazarus! Come forth!" This means we are called to rise from the dead—or perhaps, rise from *wishing* we were dead. When it's time for us to resurrect, it's not something we do on our own. Now that the Dark Night has broken us down and stripped us clean (usually to a significant level), we are more likely to be humbly open to receiving a greater quantity of Divine Presence to uplift us and Guide us. When this Presence enters our heart and soul, we now are ready to co-create a new life, with God as our Guide.

It's onward and upward from this point. It's as though the Voice of God is calling to us, saying, "I know that relationship hurt you; however, be glad, for although it was unhealthy, you learned from it. Now you know what healthy and unhealthy relationships look like and can choose the better one in your next relationship." Or Spirit might be saying, "I know you lost that job, but you didn't like it anyway. So let's co-create your soul's purpose instead."

When I let go of what I am, I become what I might be.

–Lao Tzu

For some of us, emerging from the Dark Night of the Soul might be equated to becoming a "born-again Christian." For others, it's like becoming a "born-again virgin"—someone who surrenders past sexual history in favor of starting over with a clearer sense of love, integrity, and self-worth. Whatever the case, **we usually end up feeling renewed and filled with courage and inspiration**.

19

THE ROLE OF
FORGIVENESS

When it comes to successfully rebuilding a new life, **there is nothing more effective on Earth for clearing the past and making way for a new life than the practice of forgiveness**.

The word forgiveness can be seen as synonymous with healing or a miracle. Forgiveness is both the decision to heal and/or to experience a miracle. Forgiveness defines the *outcome* of this decision to heal and experience the miracle of a shift in perception from judgment to love and from separation to oneness.

Forgiveness is experienced primarily not as a one-time event, but rather as a process. And this process generally goes through three stages: 1) We begin by forgiving others for what we believe they have done to us. 2) Then we shift towards forgiving ourselves for having judged others for what we perceived they did to us, as well as forgiving ourselves for being susceptible to what others have done. We also forgive ourselves for things we have done to ourselves. 3) The final stage of forgiveness culminates in the recognition that as we no longer choose to judge others or ourselves, we begin to experience total forgiveness for all. This allows and attracts the greatest of miracles—our awakening of Christ Consciousness.

Although the value of going through all three stages of forgiveness should be obvious, it's imperative to understand that we are not always ready to go through all three of these stages. **It's best to honor whatever level we are at in our willingness to except and experience forgiveness**. Therefore, if all we are able to muster up is a slight willingness to forgive others for the harms we perceive they've caused us, that's good enough for now. Trying to force ourselves into levels of forgiveness that we are not yet prepared to authentically experience can actually cause us more harm than good. It may place us in a state of denial and guilt that can seem overwhelming. Of course, we also need to be sensitive towards others who are not yet capable of extending forgiveness beyond their present level.

Forgiving ourselves or others does *not* mean enabling hurtful behaviors. We are *not* asked to love, trust, or forgive the ego in other people. On the contrary, it's okay to say goodbye to their ego and their egotistic behaviors. But forgiveness is not complete until we also are willing to know and affirm that beyond the person's ego is a spark of light that is as pure as God itself.

The practice of forgiveness is the most powerful gift within the heart of humankind. Forgiveness is an effective method for having our previous unhealthy patterns and belief systems—our old life—removed from our being.

This takes the physical form of actually having old neurons in the brain unplugged and re-wired with new belief systems. Such re-wiring is done by the Holy Spirit of God—if we choose to allow it.

Although there are several effective exercises/techniques for practicing forgiveness, the most basic starting point of all is simply to know that **any time a person's face, image, or name—or even the memory of an event— brings up a feeling less than peaceful and loving, it is because the soul of that person is (consciously or unconsciously) asking us to forgive them**—even if their ego doesn't realize it.

The following are some of the essentials for understanding the true definition of forgiveness:

- True forgiveness is the highest expression of love on Earth. When we truly forgive, it is an *inner* experience, whereby we access the higher self to release the misconceptions of the lower self.
- Within the human experience, there are different levels of true and false forgiveness.
- True forgiveness releases us from all limitations on, and blocks of, our ability to love unconditionally.
- All the things we think we need to forgive are symptoms of the ONE greater issue—the belief that we are separate from God and from each other.
- Patience and unconditional love are needed within the human experience to practice forgiveness effectively.

Again, the role of forgiveness cannot be overemphasized. The truth is that we can only rebuild our new life in direct proportion to our ability to forgive—ourselves and others. And although it often seems impossible to forgive some people and/or some events, **we are not asked to pretend people and things didn't cause us confusion and pain. We are only asked to realize that it was never the Light (the true self) within that person that caused us harm**, rather it was their ego (the false self) that caused the harm. Therefore, we need not forgive their ego. We need only to be willing to see and affirm the harmless Light that is buried deep within their soul.

20

BECOMING CONSCIOUS AND AWAKE

Each time we emerge from the Dark Night of the Soul (potentially leaving our unhealed and limited past behind), either we will go back to our old patterns and ways of life OR we will emerge victorious into the Light at the End of the Tunnel (healing in the present and opening to our unlimited future). **Choosing to leave behind old, unhealthy patterns, we are more awake, committed to our spiritual path, and prepared to live a life with greater Inspiration as our Guide**. This means we are waking up and becoming a more responsible, conscious person on the spiritual path. Prior to this, we may have been on the path; but it did us little good because we were unconscious.

> *The Dark Night of the Soul is a journey into light,*
> *a journey from your darkness into the strength and*
> *hidden resources of your soul.*

> –Caroline Myss

Once we begin to wake up—personally and spiritually—one of the greatest dangers remaining is the temptation to push the proverbial "snooze button." And just like those moments when we deal with our alarm clock going off in the morning, the more awake we are, the less good it will do to push the snooze button and try to go back to sleep. Still, for those of us who are only *partly* awake, the temptation is quite strong to try to ignore or minimize the lessons we hopefully have learned—trying to go back into the world as if the Dark Night were merely a bad dream that we would rather just forget about. On the other hand, if we are totally (or even mostly) awake, we usually find it *impossible* to push the snooze button. Instead, **we not only feel awake, we are even *excited* that the alarm has gone off, because *today* is a special day—it's our re-birth-day—spiritually**.

> *I awoke only to see* [that] *the rest of the world*
> *was still asleep!*
>
> –Leonardo Da Vinci

So **we need to be aware of the temptation to go back to sleep** and do all that we can to "fight the good fight" against such backsliding. It leads nowhere, other than back to creating more hell that will need to be purged away in yet another Dark Night of the Soul.

21

ACCESSING THE SPIRITUAL WARRIOR WITHIN

After emerging from the Dark Night with a greater willingness to discover who we are and to be a *conscious* participant in our lives, the next thing we have to learn is how to develop the backbone of a spiritual warrior. Being a spiritual warrior has little or nothing to do with being poised for battle nor *enjoying* a fight. Spiritual warriors actually do their best to refrain from (but not avoid) *external* confrontations and stressful encounters. Instead, they mostly engage in *internal* battles with their own ego. And yet, **whenever there is a calling to step up (on an *external* level) in a way that brings a greater good to the world, spiritual warriors answer that call.**

> *To be a spiritual warrior means to develop a special kind of courage, one that is innately intelligent, gentle, and fearless. Spiritual warriors can still be frightened, but even so they are courageous enough to taste suffering, to relate clearly to their fundamental fear, and to draw out without evasion the lessons from difficulties.*
>
> –Sogyal Rinpoche

The word "battle" (as used here) is more easily acceptable if we understand that it is not related to war, but rather is synonymous with the word "test." Therefore, to prepare for "victory in life's battles" is simply a common and more *dramatic* way of saying that we are preparing to "pass life's tests." If we focus on and engage in things that are *petty*, however, we will not have the energy, nor the clarity, to engage in what actually *does* matter. In fact, **when we allow ourselves to get hooked into *petty* things, it merely confirms that such *littleness* is our present level of consciousness**. To know whether or not to pursue a fight, it's wise to ask ourselves if the resulting good is worth the conflict. If the payoff isn't worth it, then why bother? For example, **if someone is determined to not like us, it's rarely worth trying to convince them otherwise**. Instead of waiting for their love and approval, we might just give these gifts to ourselves.

Jesus demonstrated that even physical storms can be overcome, but only when we understand that they depict our own *inner* storms and turmoil. He overcame storms by loving the conflict out of the storm. The power is not in controlling the storm on the outside but, rather, healing it on the inside. Again, **the real battles in life are *internal* battles (battles of our heart and mind)**. We should, therefore, refrain from focusing on *external*, ego-based fights and turn such conflicts into healings. The battles or tests of life are challenging us to know that any time we are not experiencing the total love and peace of God, there is a test (or opportunity) to deal with hidden wounds and issues and emerge victorious from that challenge—ending up closer to God. But if we try to *avoid* such inner challenges and wounds, the outward battles will simply return to us—although sometimes in another form and with other characters in the drama.

The basic difference between an ordinary [person]
and a warrior is that a warrior takes everything as a
challenge while an ordinary [person] *takes everything*
as a blessing or a curse.

–Carlos Castaneda

It's important, however, to remember that our purpose in stepping up to face issues (life's battles) is not for the sake of *external* victory. Instead, **we are already victorious each and every time we trust enough to step up—win or lose**. In other words, the test is often simply to see if we will stand up for what is right, or what seems to us most like peace and love. And we are never to get caught up in—nor attached to—the outcome. We are asked only to step up (instead of being afraid and immobilized) and to do our best in the given situation. We, then, are *already* victorious.

Again, most people on the spiritual path have an aversion to the concept of doing battle. But since *A Course in Miracles*, the *Koran*, and the *Bhagavad Gita* use the metaphor of a battleground to depict dealing with life's tests, who are we to argue? Lord Krishna went to battle as the guide for a gentle prince named Arjuna. Arjuna represents the hyper-passive side of us that makes every excuse to not take proper action—especially if someone else might not like it. Such people tend to get little accomplished and act like victims because they seem to always lose their battles. **Yes, it can be great to be passive, but only if that is what the moment calls for**. But if we see an accident, for example, the right thing to do is usually to help. And if we see someone in the store who is short of money, we might choose to step up and pay their bill.

Although the battle, as described in the *Gita*, is righteous, in that it is to protect a peace-loving kingdom from an evil, aggressive army; Arjuna has last minute doubts about fighting. And, as the battle begins, Arjuna cries out to Krishna for confirmation as to whether or not going to battle is the right thing to do. With tears in his eyes, Arjuna says,

"I see no value for going into battle. It seems wrong and against our religion—especially given that some of the invaders are our own family members." Krishna promptly scolds Arjuna telling him, "The very idea that you are in conflict on this matter means you are *not* accessing your Divine Mind. Get it together and take notice that there is a battle before you. Stand up and be counted. An entire kingdom of people (who will surely be destroyed) is counting on you." Krishna also advises Arjuna to, "Take control of the horses of your chariot (symbolic of the four chakras of the lower, human self) and steer your chariot (your soul) towards righteous actions. **In bringing God to the battle, you are transforming the battle into a victory—win or**

lose. Yes, it would be great to be sitting in a serene setting enjoying peace and nature, but that's *not* what's happening right NOW. In this present moment, you have to fight a good fight. So stop talking and doubting, get in your body, be a master, and get moving."

A warrior seeks to act rather than talk.

–Carlos Castaneda

Krishna also goes on to say, "Taking action is nearly always better than inactivity—provided you remain unattached to the outcome of the action. Besides, there is nothing else like a righteous battle to teach you so much about yourself—provided it is unprovoked. If you die or fail in a *righteous* battle, it matters not, because you will have grown closer to God. Of course if you succeed and arise victorious, you likely also will have gained a much better life." These *battles* that Krishna is referring to are not only battles in the world (divorce, health issues, a challenging child, etc.) but also the battles in our heart and mind (addictions, selfishness, fears, self-doubt, etc.).

Whenever a warrior decides to do something, he must go all the way, but he must take responsibility for what he does. No matter what he does, he must know first why he is doing it, and then he must proceed with his actions without having doubts or remorse about them.

–Carlos Castaneda

The *Koran* (the Holy book of the Muslims) also speaks of the necessary battle we all must fight with the ego (known as the "greater jihad")—although it's often misinterpreted and misrepresented to mean the necessity of *external* war (known as the "lesser jihad"). The *Koran* tells us to "Fight in the way of God against those who fight against you, but never be the one who begins the hostilities, for God does not love aggressors." And when Muslims *do* choose to fight, it should only be as a last resort and only in proportion to the crimes of their enemies. The *Koran* states that when an enemy asks for peace, *true* Muslims must give that peace to him. Also, the *Koran* teaches that relationships with non-Muslim nations should be peaceful.

When the prophet Mohammad and his successors went to battle, they followed clear instructions not to attack civilians—including women, children, the elderly, and religious people engaged in worship—nor were they allowed to destroy their adversary's property, crops, or animals. In other words, the *Koran* advises that we should never harm anyone or anything, although we may have to respond appropriately (within proper proportion) if someone is attempting to cause physical harm. These are nearly the same principles of a Buddhist!

Being a spiritual warrior gives us the type of courage and spiritual strength that filled Jesus during his trial and crucifixion, and it gave the forefathers of the United States the ability to take action against tyranny even though they were under threat of being hung for treason. It gave

Abraham Lincoln the ability to fight to free the slaves, and it gave Mother Theresa what she needed to go into leper colonies and trust she would somehow be guided and protected. Such courage is found in ordinary people who are choosing to be extra-ordinary.

The spiritual warrior, however, is also expressed in the woman who leaves an abusive husband even if it means she will not have his financial support for her (and possibly her children's) livelihood. Again, it means stepping up to do what's right and remaining unattached to the outcome.

22

CO-CREATING A NEW
LIFE WITH GOD

M any teachers and life coaches who want to assist us
with creating a new life fail to integrate the most
important piece of all—God's assistance. However, no matter
how much we think we know or how much experience we
have in life, it's now clear that we should no longer choose
to walk alone on our spiritual path, or try to create a new life
from this broken and limited human self. Instead, **we learn
to create events in our lives** *only* **when we are relatively
certain that such inspirations are indeed coming from
God.**

Whenever we refer to "co-creating a new life," we should
remember that there are *two* parts to this phrase: "co-creating"
and "a new life." But which part is more important: the co-
creating *or* the new life? Many teachers and life coaches who
want to help us shift into a better and happier life are focused
on the new life *itself.* The more important part, however, is
that we are *co-creating* the new life—which means that we
are surrendering and joining with God to build together
this new way of being. In so doing, our creation becomes
a spiritual manifestation and experience—more closely
mirroring who we *really* are—an extension of God.

Know to what extent the creator has honored you
above all the rest of creation. The sky is not an image
of God, nor is the moon, nor the sun, nor the beauty of
the stars, nor anything of what can be seen in creation.
You alone have been made the image of the Reality
that transcends all understanding, the likeness of
imperishable beauty, the imprint of true divinity, the
recipient of beautitude, the seal of the true light. When
you turn to him you become that which he is himself.

—Gregory of Nyasa

When we emerge into the Light after experiencing the Dark Night, **it's hardly the Divine Plan that our life continue to resemble (in any way) the *old* life that we so painfully learned to let go of**. Instead, we are now meant to be a co-creator with God—creating a life that serves the good of our soul—instead of the illusions of our ego.

What better way could there be to reach the Light at the End of the Tunnel than by *beginning* and *continuing* a relationship with God? There simply isn't a better way. In fact, **the more we grow—spiritually—the more we come to realize that we want nothing more than to have God Guiding every day of our lives**; and that the speed and effectiveness of attaining this goal depends only on the sincerity and consistency of our efforts. The results will speak for themselves soon enough, but one thing is certain: we will recognize a distinct shift within our hearts and in our lives— from fear to love and from *desperation* to *inspiration*.

Having "God Days" (days when we feel connected to God) means living a life with a greater sense of *internal* peace and inspiration and an *external* sense of health and abundance. Although we would like to assume that just being on the spiritual path will bring these blessings to us automatically, such is not necessarily the case. **Achieving a more fulfilling life involves nurturing our connection to God/Spirit in the present moment, "one day at a time."**

Nevertheless, some of us still insist on dedicating our lives to the most shallow parts of social media and various mundane activities, rather than nurturing our relationship with God. This neglect of the spiritual life results in not learning our lessons and *not* passing life's tests. This, of course, then results in those tests having to come around— yet again—often in the form of another Dark Night of the Soul. However, **just five minutes in "communion" with God can provide hours or days of inspiration.** If we take the time to develop our spiritual "muscles," they can carry us through life. But our muscles of spiritual connection must be *maintained.* When we stray from our spiritual path, it may take us only seconds to recover, yet it also could take days or even years. Communion with God allows us to bounce back sooner and with greater ease.

> *As you walk on the path of life, you must come to the realization that God is the only object, the only goal that will satisfy you.*
>
> –Paramahansa Yogananda

Starting the day by **connecting with Spirit through a simple prayer and/or meditation changes the morning, which changes the day, which changes our lives**. Starting the day in such a way, develops a sense of greater peace, inspiration, purpose, and guidance.

The process of *communing* with God is actually a combination of prayer and meditation. When we do the prayerful part of this process, the exact wording is not as important as the sincerity and humility with which we allow God to live through us—*as* us. Therefore, the general theme of this entire process (prayer and meditation, or communion with God) should be that **we are asking to be a clear channel for God's Presence on Earth—from morning till night and from night till morning**.

> *Those who* [live in communion with God] *. . . will live with renewed strength. They will soar on wings like eagles; they will run and not grow weary, they will walk and not be faint.*
>
> –Isaiah 40:31

When our communion time is complete, we then can add some visualization to the process. We might start by visualizing what kind of day would be congruent with being aligned with God/Love. Then we can let our higher mind (imagination) show us the major categories of our lives (health, relationships, finances, etc.) in a thriving state. **We should follow this visualization by confidently**

reminding ourselves that this is the kind of day we will have, as long as we don't allow our ego to interfere.

If at times we seem to lose focus and begin to slip into ego-based doubts about our new direction in life, we should do our best to see it, own it, and then make the decision to get back on course with the help of God (and the Hierarchy of Light). Even in a worst-case scenario, **all we need is a little humility and sincerity and we can turn things around**.

Change can be accomplished most of all through the power of prayer, because with God all things are possible.

–Wilfred Peterson

COMMUNING WITH GOD

Since we are not really separate from God, it's not that complicated to connect with the Heart, Mind, and Spirit of God. All we need do is to start, maintain, and end each day with the Love, Healing, and Guidance of God by calling Its Holy Presence into our heart and soul. This is accomplished through the exercise of communion. Also, it's important to reconnect with Spirit at any time possible— moment-to-moment (throughout the day)—especially when needed.

One can easily sit still an hour with closed eyes and accomplish nothing. One can as easily give God only an instant, and in that instant join with [God] completely.

—A Course in Miracles

Although communing with God is not as difficult as some would have us believe, it has a powerful and wide range of results—partly depending on our sincerity and dedication to practice. However, connecting with God anywhere from once (in the morning) to three times per day (morning, mid-day, and evening) will obviously reap the best results.

Taking our daily communion with God into a state of fulfillment involves the application of five concepts—concepts that can change our lives forever—which are as follows:

1. Mental Concentration
2. Inspirational Visualization
3. Giving Thanks
4. Inspired Actions
5. Sharing With Others

Mental Concentration is the first tool used for communing. Initially, when we engage in mental concentration for communion, it helps to select a couple of focus words (commonly referred to as a mantra). These focus words should be synonymous with God and possibly the opposite of the negative feelings we previously may have been experiencing. For example, if we felt attacked, we can call in "Safety;" if we felt confused, we can call in "Clarity;" if we felt fear of being alone, we can call in "God's Loving Embrace;" if we felt anger, we can call in "Peace."

Whatever word or two we choose (for example: "Love and Self-Worth," "Peace and Healing," "Joy and Abundance," etc.), it is imperative that we understand that these words become much like our new name or identity. Furthermore, the origin, meaning, and spiritual vibration of our new name (or new focus) will become the foundation of our New Life. Spirit, by any name, now becomes our new "core belief," which will then replace our old core issues and patterns (and their manifestations) with an entirely new, positive set of programs and perspectives, or "belief systems."

You will be called by a new name, which the mouth of the LORD will designate.

–Isaiah 62:2

Core beliefs are important because the world we see and experience is based not merely on our "thoughts," as so many teachings profess. Instead, the world we see and experience is based on the foundation of the "belief-systems" stored in our heart and soul—our higher mind. More specifically, our belief-systems are founded on, or arises from, the belief of who and what we are. Who we believe we are (either a holy being of Light or a limited, frail, and separate human being) then determines the nature of our thoughts, emotions, and experiences.

*By establishing your Source, it establishes your Identity,
and it then describes you as you must really be in truth.*

—A Course in Miracles

Inspirational Visualization is the next tool for applying our
communion. It involves imagining our mind and body being
filled with a brilliant light—the Light of God. This light also
comes from our angels, spirit guides, and soul family. This
light heals us on every level—mind, body, and soul. Then we
visualize ourselves healed and living a new life. So we see
ourselves looking, feeling, acting, and achieving that which
we desire and deserve. Remember, we are an extension of
God, which means that whatever we think upon and call
into our lives is likely to manifest, particularly because we
are now centered in our divinity and (as a co-creator) are
using the power of our mind and soul.

When concentrating and visualizing a new life, it's also
important that we include detailed visualizations of all major
categories of our life, such as health, finances, relationships,
family, and work. Additionally, when visualizing a new life,
we should forget everything we presently know about our
human selves. Within our conscious awareness, we need only
focus on and evoke Divine Presence. We then will enter a
state of consciousness beyond time, turmoil, and needs—a
state wherein we experience the answer to the prayer at the
heart of our visualization. This answer will then irresistibly
rush into our lives to manifest itself, like the most romantic
of meetings with our Higher Self.

Visualization, as a means of applying the effects of our communion with God, is far more than the typical, self-centered thoughts or "ambition-based" imaginings commonly used. The new life we are visualizing and co-creating is originating from Source, rather than from the little, separate ego-self. To assure this, it is important that what we choose to visualize is congruent with our spiritual mantra, or focus words, such as "Peace and Joy." To do so creates a certainty that Spirit is the Power behind these final, seed-planting steps.

Whatever you want to be, start to develop that pattern now.
You can instill any trend in your consciousness right now,
provided you inject a strong thought in your mind; then
your actions and whole being will obey that thought.

–Paramahansa Yogananda

Giving Thanks first helps us to lock-in whatever lessons we have learned and integrated during the Dark Night of the Soul, as well as whatever else we have accomplished along the path of life. Giving thanks is the *third* tool used to anchor in that which we have chosen as our new "reality," and is the last of the *internal* tools in this list of five. The next two tools are *external* tools to be applied. These next tools—actions and sharing—are things we do to apply the first three tools into our lives, thus anchoring them further into our being.

Give thanks for unknown blessings already on their way.

–Native American Prayer

Inspired Actions are the fourth tool we use in order to integrate our daily internal communions. This involves making sure that all of our daily actions and decisions are congruent, or in alignment, with our "focus words" and the images of our visualizations. If our focus words and visualization images are like seeds being planted in our mind and soul, then our daily actions and decisions are like food and water for those seeds. Therefore, we should choose healthy food and water that will help our seeds grow and refuse the unhealthy actions and decisions that will destroy our new seeds.

When making decisions among various possible actions, the average person often feels torn between two or more options, which equates with being caught in the world of duality, or out of touch with God's Reality of perfect Oneness. Instead, when making a decision, we can use our focus words (or mantra) to separate the valuable from the invaluable—the necessary (or best) decision from the unnecessary (or "wrong") decision. Now, with the aid of our focus words (mantra), there is only ONE option, which we discover by being in our ONE MIND—our right mind— the mind blessed by God. Now we choose only that which nurtures and feeds the seeds of our new life—our focus words. As a result of being focused, or single-minded, we reject all other options that conflict with our focus words.

*So what do we do? Anything. Something. So long as
we just don't sit there. If we screw it up, start over. Try
something else. If we wait until we've satisfied all the
uncertainties, it may be too late.*

–Lee Iacocca

Sharing With Others (the gifts or fruits of our new healing
and awakening) is the fifth and final tool for integrating our
daily communion with God. Failing to share these gifts with
others—in the form of smiles, being of service, and sharing
miracles of love and healing—may very well mean having
the fruits of our transformation "die on the vine." The Love
and Peace (or Truth) that we claim for ourselves during our
communion must be extended and shared as a means of
anchoring them into our consciousness—permanently. As
A Course in Miracles makes clear: "giving and receiving are
the same." You "receive" that which you share with others.

*He will tell you exactly what to do to help anyone He
sends to you for help, and will speak to him through
you if you do not interfere.*

–A Course in Miracles

STARTING THE DAY WITH GOD

The first sixty seconds of our day actually shapes our
experiences for the remainder of the day. We set a tone for
the day during the first sixty seconds of our waking.

The quality and content of the day's experiences are shaped largely by what is held in our mind during this transition from sleeping to waking—just as our sleep is affected by the last thoughts in our mind when we first drift off to sleep. Consequently, one of the best ways to start the day well is to immediately, upon awakening, ask God, "What would You have me do today?" Repeat this several times, slowly, and sincerely, and do your best to be open to a reply, a shift in feeling, or possibly a sense of Guidance in relation to the plan for the day. Then follow with practicing the "Communion Exercise" (noted above), which ends with giving thanks.

MAINTAINING THE DAY WITH GOD

Throughout the day, it's important to use the communion exercise to reconnect with God now and then, especially during any moments when we feel as though we have lost our center. Also, we can recognize positive synchronicities as reminders to connect with God OR as reminders that we *are* connected. In the latter instance, it's wise to give thanks that Spirit was—in that moment thanking *us* for being connected. These are the surest ways to keep our ego from controlling or sabotaging our day, as well as for realigning with Spiritual Guidance on an as-needed-basis.

ENDING THE DAY WITH GOD

No matter how well the day went and/or how often we remembered to remain connected with God, we still need to *end* the day with God. Just as it is crucial to *start* and *maintain* the day with God, it also is important to *end* the day with God. For each key event of the day, we now can review any situations or interactions with others wherein we failed to remain connected to God or act with love and kindness. Then, we can visualize the day as if we did *indeed* act differently—with more love and kindness. This helps us to download a more positive program into our soul-mind and brain. Once done, we also can review our day for any situations or interactions with others wherein we *did* remain connected to God and acted with love and kindness. We then can give thanks for each of those healthy and righteous choices. Lastly, we can end the evening process of connecting with God by stating something like the following: "Now I rest in God. I choose to surrender my sleep-time to Healing and Inspiration from the Holy Spirit of God."

23

THOSE DAMNED LEAKS

When we get on a boat to take us sailing into a new life, the last thing we want to discover is that our boat (and our lives) has leaks. Such leaks in life tend to cause us to sink—physically, emotionally, and energetically. Of course, we are not referring to leaks in the literal, physical sense. We're referring to energetic leaks caused by our own unkept promises and by our dreams that were never fulfilled. Leaks can also be caused by other people draining us—acting like psychic vampires who suck our energy (rather than our blood). Whether they happen slowly or quickly, **all energy leaks drain us on some level—leaving us feeling empty and tired.** This keeps us from following through with ideas and inspirations that could have helped us rebuild a new life.

> *You are never too old to set another goal or to dream a new dream.*
>
> –C.S. Lewis

We create leaks in our mind and in our energy field whenever we fail to complete something (dreams, projects, promises, appointments, and so forth). But we also create leaks when we allow ourselves to be hooked by the unkept promises and expectations of others—looking to receive something they, themselves, *cannot* or *will not* give.

One of the most common source of leaks comes from ideas and dreams we failed to follow-up on. Such inspirations then act like little creatures that were birthed but never brought to maturity. So they were left having to feed off of our energy field to stay alive. Therefore, in order to salvage the situation, we have to patch those leaks. And there are only two ways to do this: *follow through* with any particular ideas and projects we've started OR *let them go*.

1. **Follow Through:** Go out and bring these hopes and/or dreams to fruition—choosing to create the dreams that are inspiring and healthy—without becoming attached to the outcome. Following through with our ideas and projects involves completing them—"getting off our butts" and making them happen.

2. **Let Them Go**: Consciously choose to let some dreams go through honest recognition that you *will not* (or *cannot*) pursue those particular dreams. We create renewed energy when we allow ourselves to accept the things we cannot change. We also gain the freedom to move on with new Inspiration.

Letting go of our ideas and projects involves recognizing that there are clear signs that, although we like the fantasy of such things manifesting, we simply need to accept that they are not coming to fruition. This recognition is not easy, for it can bring up feelings of failure and/or a sense of being overwhelmed. This can be quite awkward and frustrating because if we don't step up and follow through, we have to accept the death of that dream. And as sad as this might seem, it truly pleases our ego (low self-worth) to know that if we *don't* cut this project loose, it drains our energy; and if we *do* cut it loose, we potentially will feel like we have failed—thus putting us in one of the ego's usual no-win situations.

> *It is impossible to live without failing at something,*
> *unless you live so cautiously that you might as well*
> *not have lived at all, in which case you have failed*
> *by default.*

> –J. K. Rowling

The good news, however, is that nothing truly dies. Therefore we are never truly causing harm when we choose to let things (projects, dreams, and even people) go. This means that when we release the things that cause us to have leaks, whatever original inspiration was behind these ideas and projects will either allow us to complete them OR it will draw them back to Spirit and bring them around again in a different form.

The dreams that we "*follow through*" on, actually give us energy, because we feel we have accomplished something of value and now have achieved a personal goal. The ones we truly "*let go of*" also give us energy, because the energy that was being unconsciously drained (to keep those dreams alive) now gets recycled. Either option works, but the trick is in choosing the right one at the right time.

Below is a more comprehensive list of what causes energy leaks and how to patch them:

CAUSES OF LEAKS

- Unfulfilled dreams
- Wishing and longing for things we don't have and/or can't do
- Making promises we don't keep
- Overly talking about our dreams and plans
- Receiving inspirations that become like little beings needing to be fed by their creator and, when ignored, tap into our energy systems and begin to drain us without our knowing it
- Saying things like, "I wish I had repaired my relationship with my father before he died," which is no longer possible, a waste of time, and therefore a leak

PATCHING LEAKS

- Take an inventory of all areas of your life to see what areas (such as unfulfilled dreams) hold probable leaks.
- Focus on doing what you *can* do, rather than wishing for what you *can't* do.
- Stop making promises and commitments you can't (or won't) keep.
- Do it or don't do it, but stop talking about it.

- Bid farewell to the things that are already dead. We can actually be filled up by letting things go.
- Own if something is not happening and let it go. This often gives us new-found energy. The universe recycles the energy of things to which we say goodbye.

24

REBUILDING A NEW LIFE

I t's ironic that each year people celebrate the "New Year," and yet the so-called "new" year looks pretty much the same as the *old* year (or years). However, after the emptying of the Dark Night, it's time to rebuild a new year and a new life. Additionally, **although the Dark Night tends to make us feel overwhelmed with fatigue and depression, the Light at the End of the Tunnel tends to make us feel energized with inspiration and enthusiasm**.

> We must always change, *renew, rejuvenate ourselves; otherwise, we harden.*
>
> –Johann Wolfgang von Goethe

After spending time emptying our past and patching our leaks, it's now time to refill our tank. Refilling means connecting more with God and allowing God to Guide our day and our life. The following are some good reminders for helping us to move forward in our lives:

- Keep all leaks repaired and never again allow them to accumulate.

THE DARK NIGHT OF THE SOUL

- When God downloads Its Inspiration to us, it tends to motivate and inspire us.
- Learn to follow through with inspirations, otherwise they will be taken away.
- Remember, when going in a new direction and running into obstacles, it doesn't mean you're going the wrong direction, but it certainly can reveal where we are on our path and how we are doing.
- The primary way to know if you are going in the *wrong* direction is that the goal is smaller than the obstacles.
- The primary way to know if you are going in the *right* direction is that the goal is bigger than the obstacles.

When we are not feeling connected to Spirit, **there's a chance we haven't yet done enough releasing of the past OR we have not yet adequately done our part to create a better future**. In other words, we have either neglected to *empty* our cup OR we have neglected to *refill* our cup.

The most common reasons we neglect to *empty* our cup (release the past) are as follows:

- We sometimes don't know how.
- We are overwhelmed by fear of change.
- What is familiar has become our habituated behavior.
- We neglect working on the cellular memory that needs clearing.
- We are not using progressive (outside of the box) methods for clearing.

The most common reasons we neglect to *refill* our cup (co-create a new life) are as follows:

• We have not sufficiently healed the past (and/or not patched our leaks).
• We are not refilling our cup with new Inspiration each day through communion (prayer and meditation) exercise.
• We are not applying enough positive thinking and affirmations.
• We have not made a clear enough list of things we are ready to manifest.
• We are failing to see/feel/experience God as being close enough to help us.

There are several things we can do to nurture our refilling or rebuilding stage, but two of the most important things are as follows:

1. Repeat positive affirmations (preferably aloud) such as, "I release all limiting former beliefs about who I am and what I deserve in my life, and I deny the effects of my past." Also, think and speak only positive words, doing away with mental and verbal negativity.
2. Learn to deal with thoughts and fears the way a warrior deals with going into battle or the way a spiritual master seeks to deal with any challenge— "divide and conquer." Make it a habit to confront and heal any issues or unhealthy patterns that arise. Look at them head-on and dismantle them and their power by asking such questions as:

"Is this problem as real and present as I believe it to be?"

"Is my reaction coming from love or fear?"

"If the worst case scenario actually happened, what am I really afraid of?"

> *Take the first step in faith. You don't have to see the whole staircase, just take the first step.*
>
> –Martin Luther King

Such courage and clarity is what it takes for true co-creators to see the fruits within the new life that potentially awaits us all.

25

BECOMING A
LIVING MASTER

After we have spent an adequate amount of time acclimating to living in the Light, we are taken to another level of consciousness—being a living master. This is not to be confused with an "Ascended Master." Instead, this refers to a person who has passed through the Dark Night of the Soul and now chooses to maintain at least a reasonable amount of their center and integrity while still remaining in a physical body. They choose to maintain their trust in the process of focusing on spiritual truths—even while living in the material world. Living masters choose to be responsible enough to *learn* the lessons of the past, rather than *judging* themselves for the past.

Religion is for people who fear hell, but spirituality is
for those who have been there!

–Unknown

Living masters look somewhat the same as everyone else, having no special outfit or uniform, and yet they are quite different indeed. They do not try to act superior, nor *are* they truly superior. They are different mainly on the *inside* (which is reflected in their outer actions), because they *externally* put into practice that which they have achieved *internally*. **Living Masters are different from most people in that their first priority is the practice of love and forgiveness.** Their other priorities include the following:

- Being helpful and of service in all ways possible.
- Being responsible for their own life and decisions.
- Being Divinely Guided in actions and decisions.
- Being committed to living a life of healthiness and making the healthiest decisions possible.

Living masters tend to maintain a balance between stillness and movement or action and passivity. Therefore, **if we want to experience the fullness of a new life (after completing the process of the Dark Night of the Soul), it's essential that we neither overly procrastinate nor overly get caught up in planning and controlling.** However, for those who choose to be excessively passive, there is also a danger in remaining stagnant or remaining a "victim" of a world that passes them by.

It is hard to give unlimited power to limited minds.

–Nikola Tesla

There are times when people attempt to start something but then, after the first delay or obstacle, say: "I guess it's not meant to be . . ." Such people are not living masters and do not understand the Laws of Spirit, nor the principles of mastery. The odds are that they will not fully discover the new life they were hoping for, which means they are likely to fall back into the same pattern as their former life, that is, until the Dark Night comes back to take them once again through the crucible of transformation.

The way to get started is to quit talking and begin doing.

–Walt Disney

After all, how many times have you heard of a great master, teacher or leader (such as Jesus, Buddha, Moses, etc.) saying: "Oh well, I guess it's not meant to be . . . !"? The answer is NEVER!!! No great teacher or leader would say such a thing, and yet such comments are inexplicably common among the so-called "spiritual people" of today.

26

DISCOVERING YOUR SOUL'S PURPOSE

Once we recognize that we have clearly entered the Light at the End of the Tunnel, **we will go through stages of developing such personal attributes as becoming more fully alive, becoming more consciously aware, accessing our inner spiritual warrior, and awakening our inner master** (to some new level). Also, we will now begin to bring the Light of God into the lives of all others on Earth—particularly through the form of fulfilling our soul's purpose.

> *To be alive is to be on fire with purpose, to move forward with undaunted determination toward a goal.*
>
> –Paramahansa Yogananda

Edgar Cayce once said that **human beings cannot truly feel complete without knowing their soul's purpose**. The good news is that we don't have to look very far for our purpose: Everyone has the same soul's purpose, which is to bring the Light of God into this world. But we all do have a unique manner in which we will *express* that purpose, and *that* is what we are here on Earth to discover.

*One thing I want to make clear, as far as my
own rebirth is concerned, the final authority
is myself and no one else.*

–Dalai Lama

Although we cannot—in this limited space—completely cover the topic of our soul's purpose, there are a few key questions we all can ask ourselves that will help unlock this seeming mystery. Suggestions that might help us to discover our soul's purpose include the following:

- Ask yourself what talents people most complimented you on throughout your life. Chances are, they were unconsciously seeing your soul's purpose even before *you* did.
- Consider having an astrological and/or numerological chart done specifically focusing on your soul's purpose to see what these charts say and how they compare with what others have told you, as well as with your own list of gifts. [Note: We have such charts in our online store on our website.]
- Make a list of a dozen of your greatest gifts and then try to narrow the list down to just five or six items. This list might include gifts like: teacher, healer, green thumb, good with children, loves nature, and so on.
- Discovering our soul's purpose is not unlike developing a mission statement for a business. The only difference is that this is a *"personal"* mission

statement. So once you are done with the steps in these first suggestions, try to blend the words that represent your greatest gifts into your personal mission statement. Various examples of possible personal mission statements (your soul's purpose) include:

- Guiding others towards personal fulfillment through inner healing.
- Using art to encourage others to open up to their creativity.
- Teaching children about God through nature.
- Guiding people through times of transition.
- Using sports to teach children the value of teamwork.

Lastly, once you get an idea of what you might end up doing as your soul's purpose, for it to materialize successfully, you need to answer affirmatively these three qualifications: 1) Do you love what you do? 2) Are you good at it? 3) Is it something people want or need? If you can say yes to each of these questions, then the likelihood of success is fairly certain. But remember, **do not assume that having an inspiration means your soul's purpose will automatically result in *external* success**. Indeed, quite often, when Spirit seems to promise us success, such success is to manifest *internally*, rather than *externally*.

For example, despite all his dedication and hard work, even Moses did not enter the "Promised Land" on a physical level. But he did indeed enter spiritually—thus becoming an "Ascended Master" when he reached the other side.

So, remain patient and keep peace and happiness as your emotional compass through life. This is your most certain means of knowing, that when it comes to discovering your soul's purpose, you are moving in the right direction.

There is perfection in the journey that is not obvious
until the end of the journey.

–Alan Cohen

SUMMARY & CONCLUSION

As has been explained, the *Dark Night of the Soul* describes only *half* of the total journey of the "Soul Transformation Process." The other half is the *Light at the End of the Tunnel*. The entire process is also referred to as the "hero's journey" because **it takes such courage to walk through this challenging initiation**. Unfortunately, however, some people seem to lack the courage, wisdom, strength, tenacity, and/or knowledge (or insight) to complete this journey. But, **since, ultimately, we are the ones who are calling for and designing this journey—personalizing it to our needs—we obviously must also have whatever it is that we need to get through it**. All we have to do is believe in ourselves and the process. Adding the Strength and Will of God to support us, we can be *certain* we do indeed have everything we need to make it to the Light at the End of the Tunnel.

> *There are two mistakes one can make along the road to truth . . . not going all the way, and not starting.*
>
> *—Buddha*

As we exit the Dark Night of the Soul and enter the Light at the End of the Tunnel, the experience of being in the Dark Night will, like a nightmare, begin to fade away—with its details seeming almost surreal, as though it happened to someone else. But rather than taking it for granted and ignoring the lessons, **we, as masters, will forever remember what we learned during the Dark Night, so that such lessons need not return**.

Learning from, and passing, life's tests is what we are here to do. We all have heard stories and seen movies of heroes and heroines who seem to have a normal life, and then they are pulled into the journey called "life." They are thrust into self-discovery and inner purging (the Dark Night). This is usually the part of the story or movie where the hero/heroine is feeling deflated, hopeless, and exhausted— sometimes even feeling enraged at God. Eventually, however, they end up victorious (the Light at the End of the Tunnel). This is usually the part of the story or movie where the hero/ heroine is seen finding true love, being crowned into royalty, or shouting with happiness with their arms outstretched towards the heavens.

> *All human events are rooted in the law of cause and effect ... In this life you are the architect of your own destiny.*
>
> –Paramahansa Yogananda

Again, the Dark Night of the Soul *and* the Light at the End of the Tunnel are usually portraying the archetypal hero/heroine's journey. When we go through the Dark Night, however, it is now *our* journey—*we* are the hero or heroine. *This* is the destiny of us all—either sooner or later—and **we are the ones who decide when to be the master who emerges victorious from life's tests**. The stories of Sleeping Beauty, Perseus, Beowulf, Thecla, and Odysseus are all stories of characters (historic or not) who are showing us how to transcend life's tests so that we may return to the Light from which we came—becoming the pure Light that God created us to be.

> *No eye has seen, no ear has heard, no mind has conceived what God has prepared for those who return to Love.*
>
> −1 Corinthians 2:9

APPENDIX A

PRAYERS DURING THE
DARK NIGHT OF THE SOUL

*I fear not . . . for the Spirit of God goes with me; He will
not fail me or forsake me.* —Deuteronomy 31:6

*I will not fear nor obsess on matters that are beyond my
understanding. Instead, I choose to be still and quiet myself,
just as a small child can quiet itself when held against its
mother.* —Psalm 131:1-2

*Why am I afraid and down in the dumps? I fixed my eyes
on God, and soon I'll be praising Him and smiling again.*
—Psalm 42:5

*I can withstand all forms of attack, as I am firm in my
faith . . . knowing that everyone in the world goes through
the same kinds of tests.* —I Peter 5:9

*In Christ I have peace and confidence. In the world I have
challenges and tests; but I can be happy and certain! For
Christ has overcome the world.* —John 16:33

*I do not yet see things clearly. But it will not be long before
the weather clears and the sun shines brightly! I will see it all
then, as clearly as God sees! In the meantime, I have three
things to guide me: trust, hope, and most importantly, love.*
—I Corinthians 13:10-13

Though I am surrounded by challenges, God will preserve me against all forms of attack. He will strengthen me against those who hate me. His power will save me. The Lord will work out his plans for my life. —Psalm 138:7-8

No weapon formed against me shall succeed, and every tongue that speaks against me with judgment shall be proven wrong. This is my inheritance because I am a holy child of God. —Isaiah 54:17

God comforts, encourages, and supports me in every situation. God also enables me to support others who need comfort. —II Corinthians 1:4

I will not lose heart, for in due time I will succeed, as long as I do not give up. —Galatians 6:9

Blessed am I when I am patient and stand firm through my tests, for then I will receive the crown of life which God has promised. —James 1:12

I stand peacefully before God, waiting for guidance and salvation. Why then should I be tense with fear when troubles come? —Psalm 62:1-2

The things I plan may not happen right away. But slowly, steadily, surely, the time approaches when my destiny will be fulfilled. If it seems slow, I do not despair, for these things will surely come to pass. I will just be patient! —Habakkuk 2:3

APPENDIX B

PRAYERS DURING THE
LIGHT AT THE END OF THE TUNNEL

God now wipes away every tear from my eyes, and loss
[the Dark Night] *shall be no more; neither shall there be*
mourning, nor crying, nor pain anymore; for the former things
have passed away. —Revelation 21:4

With God's help I can advance against a troop and can scale
a wall into victory. —Psalm 18:29

My weeping lasted all night, but now my joy arrives as a
new dawn breaks. —Psalm 30:5

I waited patiently and expectantly for the Lord; and He heard
my cry. He lifted me up out of a horrible pit of mud and set
my feet upon a rock, steadying my steps and guiding my
movements. —Psalm 40:1-3

I arise from the depression where my circumstances have kept
me—I arise to a new life! I shine . . . for my light has come,
and the glory of God has risen upon me! —Isaiah 60:1

I set my mind and keep it set on higher things, not on the
things of this world. —Colossians 3:2

The Spirit of God has turned my morning into joyful
dancing and has taken away my clothes of mourning and,
instead, clothed me with joy. —Psalm 30:11-12

I am constantly renewed in my spirit and mind, and I choose to embody my Christ Self. –Ephesians 4-24

As I align with Christ Consciousness, I am born anew: The old has gone, the new is here! –II Corinthians 5:17

I know that God has a plan for me . . . plans for me to prosper and be safe, plans to give me hope and a bright future." –Jeremiah 29:11

I learned my lessons with regard to my former way of life. I have put off my old self, to be made new in my thoughts and beliefs; embodying my new self, created in God's Holy Image. –Ephesians 4:22-24

I release the former things, so as not to dwell on the past. I am focusing on my new life that now springs forth! God has now made a way for me through the wilderness and has made streams in the wasteland. –Isaiah 43:18-19

God has made everything beautiful in its time. –Ecclesiastes 3:11

The Holy Spirit has removed my heart of stone and has placed a new heart and a new spirit within me. –Ezekiel 36:26

Whom have I in heaven but God? And there is nothing on Earth that I desire besides God. My flesh and my heart may seem limited, but God gives me a heart and mind of unlimited power. –Psalm 73:25-26

And though my beginning [Dark Night] *was small, my latter days* [at The End of the Tunnel] *will be great.* –Job 8:7

5-DAY INTENSIVES
with Michael Mirdad

 **MASTERY
& HEALING**

This intensive is great for anyone who
is ready to discover new levels of direction, responsibility, balance,
wholeness, and a life of fulfillment, as well as learning how to bring
God and all spiritual learning into their daily lives and activities. It
teaches how to experience the best life possible in every aspect of
living. No other single event offers so much! Topics include physical
mastery–manifesting prosperity, living healthy through yoga and diet,
and training in several healing arts; emotional mastery–developing
psychic abilities, creating fulfilling relationships, and learning advanced
emotional healing techniques; mental mastery–developing greater
focus, learning effective meditation, and discovering your soul's
purpose; and spiritual mastery–developing a life plan, learning true
forgiveness, awakening higher levels of consciousness, and opening
your heart center.

 **AWAKENING
CHRIST CONSCIOUSNESS**

This intensive is for students and teachers of Christ Consciousness.
It teaches attendees to connect with their True (Christ) Self and
deeper levels of spiritual awareness. It covers advanced teachings
and spiritual concepts, as well as profound levels of application. This
program includes initiations into Christ Consciousness through
rarely understood mystery teachings of Jesus–some of which were
transferred to Mary Magdalene, clearing of various energy centers
(chakras), the secret teachings of Christ, Jesus' missing years amongst
the Essenes and the Mystery Temples, and experiencing your own
spiritual baptism.

Other Books by Grail Press

Healing the
Heart & Soul

Michael Mirdad
$15.00

The Heart of
*A Course In
Miracles*

Michael Mirdad
$20.00

You're Not Going
Crazy...You're Just
Waking Up!

Michael Mirdad
$15.00

An Introduction
to Tantra and
Sacred Sexuality

Michael Mirdad
$15.00

The Seven
Initiations on the
Spiritual Path

Michael Mirdad
$15.00

Creating
Fulfilling
Relationships

Michael Mirdad
$15.00

The Book of Love
and Forgiveness

Michael Mirdad
$15.00

Mother Mary
and the Undoing
Process

Robin Rose
$15.00

To order any of our books or request more information on any of
these publications, please call our office **(360) 671–8349** or visit
www.MichaelMirdad.com for a complete list of books, CDs, and DVDs.

Order Form

To order any of our books or request more information on any of these publications, please call our office or visit our website for a complete list of books, CDs, and DVDs.

Book Titles

The Book of Love and Forgiveness
_____ copies at $15.00 each =   _____

Healing the Heart & Soul
_____ copies at $15.00 each =   _____

Creating Fulfilling Relationships
_____ copies at $15.00 each =   _____

The Heart of _A Course In Miracles_
_____ copies at $20.00 each =   _____

An Introduction to Tantra and Sacred Sexuality
_____ copies at $15.00 each =   _____

Mother Mary and the Undoing Process
_____ copies at $15.00 each =   _____

Seven Initiations of the Spiritual Path
_____ copies at $15.00 each =   _____

You're Not Going Crazy...You're Just Waking Up!
_____ copies at $15.00 each =   _____

Add $2.50 for S/H per book   _____

Total   _____

Grail Productions • PO Box 1908 • Sedona, AZ 86339
(360) 671-8349 • office@grailproductions.com
www.MichaelMirdad.com

About the Author

Michael Mirdad is a world-renowned spiritual teacher, healer, and author with an extensive background in spirituality and healing. He is the author of the best-selling books *Healing the Heart & Soul, Sacred Sexuality: A Manual for Living Bliss*, and *You're Not Going Crazy . . . You're Just Waking Up!* Michael is regularly featured as a keynote speaker at some of the world's largest conferences, as well as being on radio, television, and various Internet programs. In addition to being a cover story in Evolve Magazine, Michael has been featured in such magazines as *Yoga Journal*, *Sedona Journal*, and *Whole Self Times*.

Michael has traveled throughout the world conducting thousands of classes, lectures, and workshops on spirituality, relationships, and healing. He is one of the few teachers in the Western world with over 30 years of tantric teaching and practice and is the creator of "Spiritual Tantra" and "Middle-Path Tantra."

Michael's powerful and insightful private sessions have transformed the lives of thousands of clients. His vast knowledge and wisdom combined with his personal warmth, humor, and integrity have earned him the title of "Teacher's Teacher" and "Healer's Healer" from students, teachers, and authors around the world.